Feeling Good by Doing Good

Feeling Good by Doing Good

A Guide to Authentic Self-Esteem and Well-Being

CHRISTOPHER J. MRUK

OXFORD
UNIVERSITY PRESS

OXFORD
UNIVERSITY PRESS

Oxford University Press is a department of the University of Oxford. It furthers
the University's objective of excellence in research, scholarship, and education
by publishing worldwide. Oxford is a registered trade mark of Oxford University
Press in the UK and certain other countries.

Published in the United States of America by Oxford University Press
198 Madison Avenue, New York, NY 10016, United States of America.

Library of Congress Cataloging-in-Publication Data
Names: Mruk, Christopher J., author.
Title: Feeling good by doing good : a guide to authentic
self-esteem and well-being / Christopher J. Mruk.
Description: New York, NY : Oxford University Press, [2019] |
Includes bibliographical references.
Identifiers: LCCN 2018008295 | ISBN 9780190637163 (hardcover) |
ISBN 9780190669508 (epub)
Subjects: LCSH: Self-esteem. | Well-being.
Classification: LCC BF697.5.S46 M778 2018 | DDC 158.1—dc23
LC record available at https://lccn.loc.gov/2018008295

9 8 7 6 5 4 3 2 1

Printed by Sheridan Books, Inc., United States of America

CONTENTS

This book is different from others I have written in at least two ways. First, most of my writing addresses scholarly audiences, especially fellow social scientists and researchers. As such, the material involves original research and the development of fairly rigorous empirical arguments. There is real value in such work, of course, but it appeals to a very limited audience. This new book is intended to be more practical to reach a larger group of readers, namely, mental health professionals, many of their clients, and those in the general public who wish to learn more about authentic self-esteem and how it helps increase well-being.

Second, this book is in some ways the one I have always wanted to write. As a clinical psychologist coming from a good working-class family in which mental illness happened to run, I frequently wondered how different our lives would have been if we (my family as well as psychology in general because we turned to it for help) had known more about real, healthy, and positive—that is, authentic—self-esteem. Although that did not occur for us, I have seen it make a genuine positive difference for clients and students over the years. Understanding the value of authentic self-esteem and seeing the ways in which it helps people increase their personal and interpersonal well-being is what prompted me to devote a book to this subject.

Suffice it to say in an introductory sense that authentic self-esteem has to do with how people face certain challenges in life. Research on these *self-esteem moments*, as I call them, always seems to involve facing a problem or dilemma that can be solved in one of two ways. The first might be best described as healthy because it is virtuous or good, and the other alternative can be called unhealthy, of lesser worth, or poor. In other words, the big secret of authentic self-esteem is that it is earned, not given, because this way of feeling good about oneself only comes after trying one's best to do one's best. That extra effort, it turns out, often makes a big difference.

It might seem that talking about authentic self-esteem in more applied or everyday language should be easier than meeting the demands of a scholarly or scientific audience, but I have found that is not the case. Trying to describe things like the functions of self-esteem, its four basic types, how self-esteem develops, the connection between well-being and self-esteem, not to mention how to change it in everyday language, actually push one's envelope of understanding. Creating examples to show how a concept works in real life or developing activities that have practical value in the real world requires more than meets the eye. It is my hope that the 30 years I've worked on researching self-esteem and helping increase it in healthy ways offers something to the more general audience for whom this book was written.

ACKNOWLEDGMENTS

Books are written by an individual or a small number of them. But like most things in life, they actually involve many people. Thus, one real pleasure extended to authors is the opportunity to name and thank some of the people involved in the process. First and foremost, of course, I always mention my wife, Marsha. Among other things, she is an impressive mental health professional who has lived with a high degree of authentic self-esteem and genuinely positive psychology all of her life. As a Vice President of Behavioral Health for the Firelands Regional Medical Center, she directs some seven counties of community mental health services in Ohio, something that demonstrates her strong belief that everyone should have access to quality mental health care regardless of income.

In addition, it is important to acknowledge the people who have accompanied me in my writing journey so far, especially my family of origin (Veronica, Joseph, and Steven Mruk), and my second family (Dee Mruk, Pam Bradshaw, and Tina Waid, as well as Carl, Sylvia, and Virginia Oliver). I am more than fortunate to have Karen Osterling, John Moor, Emma Millis, and JoEtta Crupi as readers who helped improve the flow of the book. Similarly, it is important to express appreciation to Rich and Marielle Aimes, as well as Michelle Fillmore, who "tried out" the manuscript to see if its suggestions were clear and workable. Next, come a few close friends who always seemed to be with me as I stumbled along in life, often not doing it right but always learning. Thanks for helping to pick up the pieces from time to time, Tony Barton, Bob and Pam Harmount, Joan Hartzell, Pete and Marsha Kowalski, Bob Noe, and Frank and Maryann Salotti.

On a more professional note, I am pleased to say that the fine people at Springer Publishing Company, New York, have allowed me to reuse here some material from the books on self-esteem and positive psychology I have developed with them over the years, especially the most recent edition of *Self-esteem and Positive Psychology: Research, Theory, and Practice* (fourth edition; 2013). Equally pleasing is that Oxford University Press, one of the oldest and most respected publishing houses in the world, saw value in an applied version of my work. Issac D Priyakumar kindly guided me through their production process. Sarah Harrington deserves special recognition in this regard because not only was she instrumental in making the contract happen, but she also gave considerable time and energy working with me as a writer to make the book a better one. In some very real ways, Sarah, the book is a collaborative effort and thank you for the help.

Finally, it is important to say a word to the undergraduate and graduate students I have had the privilege of working with over the years at Bowling Green State University. Their willingness to explore with me many of the ideas found in this book before they were developed enough to appear in print was the most exciting part of the process. As I often say at the beginning of an exam, "May the Force be with you" when facing the challenges of living that are discussed in the following pages!

LIST OF FIGURES, TABLES, AND BOXES (ILLUSTRATIONS AND THOUGHT ACTIVITIES)

Feeling Good by Doing Good

What Is Authentic Self-Esteem
and Why Does It Matter?

INTRODUCTION

Today many social scientists, mental health professionals, and laypersons know that self-esteem is connected to well-being or the lack thereof in at least three important ways. One is that problematic forms of self-esteem, such as low and defensive self-esteem, are associated with many negative personal and interpersonal phenomena. In reviewing research on self-esteem over the past several decades, for example, Mark Leary and Geoff MacDonald (2003) found that in regard to general or trait self-esteem,

> People with lower trait self-esteem tend to experience virtually every aversive emotion more frequently than people with higher self-esteem. Trait self-esteem correlates negatively with scores on measures of anxiety . . . sadness and depression . . . hostility and anger . . . social anxiety . . . shame and guilt . . . embarrassability . . . and loneliness . . . as well as general negative affectivity and neuroticism. (pp. 404–405)

Although one might quibble about the phrase *virtually every aversive emotion*, the point is that self-esteem is certainly involved in a host of problems of living. Indeed, it is even mentioned as a factor in some 24 mental health disorders (O'Brien, Bartoletti, & Leitzel, 2006). This characteristic of self-esteem alone makes knowing more about it a worthwhile endeavor.

Another major connection between self-esteem and well-being is that newer work shows how self-esteem is also connected to important positive phenomena. For example, now we know that self-esteem is involved in such things as happiness, relationship satisfaction, and one's ability to reach his or her optimal level of personal or interpersonal well-being (Diener & Diener, 1995; Kernis, 2003). In fact, even the most severe critics of self-esteem are forced by data to admit that high self-esteem allows people to better handle stress, something that is necessary to effectively cope with life's problems (Baumeister, Campbell, Krueger, & Vohs, 2003).

The third vital connection between self-esteem and well-being concerns how people fare in their lives over time, which makes self-esteem a major developmental issue. This dimension of self-esteem may be most strongly active in what are called *self-esteem moments,* or the times in life when one's self-esteem is called into question by a certain type of challenge. It typically involves being in a situation or facing a problem that requires an individual to choose between two alternatives. One of them may be described as *good* in that it involves taking the higher road in regard to the merit, value, or worth of the choice but also requires some degree of competence or even courage to enact. The other is *poor* in that it involves a lesser or even unhealthy choice that is much easier to make because it requires little work and no courage at all. I will describe these challenges of living in more detail throughout the book, but for now it is only important to know that these choices affect self-esteem in either a positive or negative way, depending on which path the person takes, and that they have a cumulative impact on one's identity and well-being over time.

THE CASE OF M

One way to illustrate the connections between self-esteem and well-being is through the use of examples and case studies. Examples are helpful because they may occur at any point in a book that a key concept is presented or discussed. Consequently, I offer many examples to show how self-esteem works in everyday life. Case studies are especially helpful when working with a developmental process because they can show how experience and behavior change over time. If a case study is to be used in this way, it is often best to introduce it at the beginning so that readers can develop a sense of how development occurs.

Although we did not meet until later in her life when she began to have trouble feeling capable at work and with being valued in her relationships, M first showed signs of having difficulty with competence, worthiness, and happiness around age 8. Such details as current age, ethnicity, educational level, and other socioeconomic factors are not presented because they vary from person to person, though it may be helpful to imagine them if desired. What makes her story helpful for understanding self-esteem and well-being was not even her diagnosis, which involved depression and anxiety, or her particular problems as they are far from unusual in clinical work. Rather, M's extremely good memory of her childhood coupled with an ability to effectively describe events related to the process of human development are useful here because they illustrate much of what we know about how self-esteem and well-being actually work.

She readily recalled, for example, how she doubted her own abilities to succeed enough that she consistently held back her best efforts when they could have made a positive difference. Rather than take a chance and participate in a game or to try hard to win one as a child, she recounted how consistently she would avoid the challenge or only make a half-hearted attempt. The result, of course, was often being left out or frequently experiencing failure, either of which confirmed growing fears of inadequacy concerning her competence as a person. She also described going down a negative interpersonal path with an older cousin during adolescence out of an excessive fear of rejection. M found that this type of choice resulted in several difficult, perhaps even traumatic, interpersonal events that made her feel unworthy. Finally, she seemed to have enough insight to recognize how early in life she began to avoid responsibility for her own actions by blaming negative events on others. Although this and similar tactics may have reduced some pain at the time, they also began to trap her ability to take risks, try new alternatives, stand up for herself, and grow.

M knew that her parents were aware of these issues and that they tried their best to help her. For example, they realized that small failures distressed M more than her siblings or playmates and often attempted to cheer her up by suggesting she look at the bright side or deal with negative feelings by moving on to something else. However, instead of taking such care to heart, M experienced these efforts as further proof of her inadequacy or worthlessness and pushed away these and other sources of assistance or acceptance. In other words, rather than trying to break free of negative thinking and self-defeating behavior, slowly but surely M traveled down the road that made her vulnerable to several classic self-esteem traps. These traps, it will be shown later, are habits of mind and behavior that result in a loss of competence, worthiness, and authentic self-esteem.

Over time, her problematic self-esteem themes developed fully enough in adulthood to create anxiety about her competence at work and depression concerning her sense of worth in relationships. Eventually, these problems of living became painful enough that she finally sought help, which prompted M to call for an appointment. The most unfortunate thing about this case is not that M had difficulties managing self-esteem, as many people struggle to maintain a healthy sense of competence and worth. Rather, the sad thing is that it took M so long to do something about it, because breakthroughs in the psychology of self-esteem and in positive psychology could have made a very significant difference for her long before reaching this painful point. Accordingly, the following pages examine different types of self-esteem, its basic functions, various self-esteem problems, the development of self-esteem, the way self-esteem works in relationships, and, most important, how to increase authentic self-esteem and, therefore, well-being.

THE IMPORTANCE OF DEFINITIONS

People have been talking about self-esteem for a long time. The term itself is over 350 years old, so it is not surprising that most people assume they know what it means. Similarly, most of us realize that a healthy degree of self-esteem is better than a lack of it and that poor self-esteem is associated with negative conditions, such as those mentioned earlier, and a lack of well-being. What many people do not understand, however, is that this vital dimension of human life can be defined in at least three very different ways and that only one of them involves what some of us in the field call *authentic self-esteem*. In other words, it is never a good idea to assume that people mean the same thing when they discuss self-esteem.

Failing to define something as complex as self-esteem before engaging with the concept will almost always result in confusion, misunderstanding, or worse. For example, depending on how one defines it, some people extol the virtues of self-esteem, while others regard it as a form of egotistical self-love. Indeed, some social scientists even focus on what they call the *dark side* of self-esteem, which shows up in such things as false pride, narcissism, or even aggression (Baumeister, Campbell, Krueger, & Vohs, 2003). Authentic self-esteem, I hope to show, is none of these things, so it is very important to take time to discuss what that self-esteem is and is not before going much further.

Of course, self-esteem is not the only term that suffers from this problem. In fact, the issue of defining what one means by a key term is quite common when people try to understand human behavior. Imagine, for instance, the damage that could be done in the following scenario depicting another definitional failure. Let us say that as a psychologist, I found a treatment that works very well for helping my depressed clients. Then, I go on to write about this new method in a scientific journal and other clinicians begin to use those techniques with their clients. Let us also assume the practitioners take great care to follow each step and do so correctly. However, later we are all shocked to find that although the suicide rate for my depressed patients was zero, the rate for these other practitioners' clients had tragically skyrocketed. The important question is, of course, what went wrong here?

The answer is deceptively simple. By assuming that everyone understands depression in the same way, I neglected to tell readers that all of my clients were relatively healthy, young, intelligent, and moneyed college students who were a little sad because they had a weekend without a date or received a low grade on an exam. This population responds well to almost any type of intervention and these problems are minor ones. The problem is that if the other clinicians were treating clients who were severely depressed, economically poor, sometimes psychotic, and suffering a high degree of suicidal risk to begin with, using my techniques might prove completely useless or even harmful. If I had simply followed good scientific practice, I would have told my colleagues what I had actually meant by depression, which in this case was just feeling blue but being in pretty good shape otherwise. Then, as clinicians, they could evaluate the information more accurately and decide whether or not it was appropriate to try my techniques with their more seriously depressed populations, or at least to take appropriate precautions when doing so.

In science, we call this basic step *operationalizing* a definition, which means taking care to define key terms precisely so that others know what we mean by them and then using those terms in a way that is consistent throughout the work. Taking the time to examine the three major ways that social scientists, therapists, and others may define self-esteem creates two advantages. First, it reduces the type of confusion I just mentioned. Second, it allows us to more clearly focus on identifying, discussing, and perhaps even enhancing authentic self-esteem.

The great English writer and poet John Milton (1642/1950) is often credited with coining the term *self-esteem* in 1642. He appears to have used it while standing up for his work after reading what he felt was an unjust criticism of it, a criticism that may have gone so far as to question his integrity as a person as well as an author. Later Milton deepened the concept in his epic work *Paradise Lost* (1667/1931), which discusses, among many other things, self-esteem in relation to doing that which is just and right when necessary. It may be illuminating to remember that during this period many, if not most, human qualities were discussed in a biblical context. Consequently, it might be said that the original use of the term tied self-esteem to moral issues as well as practical matters. This view of the concept considerably elevates it from the way self-esteem is usually used today and is something we will explore further from a scientific perspective at the end of the book.

The first great American psychologist William James (1890/1983) brought the concept of self-esteem to the field of psychology over 200 years later. James was interested in the development of the self and saw self-esteem as an important part of this process, especially in regard to establishing and maintaining one's sense of identity as a person over time. Since then, self-esteem became the third most studied covariate (variable) in social psychology during the 1990s, following work on gender issues and the study of negative affect, which includes such things as depression, anxiety, anger, and the like (Rodewalt & Tragakis, 2003). Today, of course, the term is also commonly used in the context of parenting, education, and popular culture.

Despite this very substantial background, the fact of the matter is that many people, both lay and professional alike, question the value of self-esteem as a concept and sometimes even criticize its use. For example, in the last part of the 20th century a group of social scientists claimed that self-esteem had little value because it did not predict much of anything in their work, even though they admitted that self-esteem does correlate with happiness and can act as a buffer against stress. Others suggested that self-esteem is the outcome of behavior, not a cause of it, because self-esteem is something people feel only after something else occurs, such as solving a problem or being praised by another. And still others, especially in popular media, saw self-esteem as an excessive focus on the self, something akin to narcissism or a form of self-worship and perhaps even sinful. All of these criticisms, it turns out, are both a little right and very wrong (Mruk, 2013a).

Defining Self-Esteem as a Form of Competence

William James (1890/1983) defined self-esteem in the following way: "Self-Esteem = Success/Pretentions" (p. 296), which in today's terms means that self-esteem is a ratio between one's achievements on one hand, and one's goals on the other. This *discrepancy definition*, as it is sometimes called, indicates that the closer an individual comes to reaching his or her goals, the better the person feels about himself or herself. Those who do well in this regard are said to have positive self-feelings or high self-esteem, and those who do not live up to their aspirations struggle with negative self-feelings or low self-esteem.

This definition is not as simple as it may look at first. For instance, James made it very clear that success alone does not necessarily affect self-esteem. Rather, it is being successful in the areas of life that matter to a person that are important, especially the domains tied to one's sense of identity. James (1890/1983, p. 296) used the examples of a pugilist and a psychologist to make this point. To paraphrase, if I see myself as a boxer, then how I perform in that domain of life is important for my identity. Doing well in the ring affirms my identity because reaching my goals there makes me feel good about myself, which results in high self-esteem. Doing poorly in the ring, of course, has the opposite effect. However, I may also happen to be a good psychologist but do not care about psychology very much. Consequently, success or failure in this arena does not involve my identity and, therefore, means little for self-esteem. The situation would be quite reversed if I saw myself as a psychologist but not as a boxer. This basic self-esteem dynamic applies to any area of life that is tied to a person's identity, such as being a good worker, friend, colleague, parent, homemaker, card player, musician, golfer, and so on. Later we will see that there are six domains of living everyone faces throughout the life cycle that are connected to self-esteem and identity in this way.

The definition of self-esteem as a form of success, or *competence* as certain developmental psychologists call it (White, 1959), dominated the fields of psychology and psychiatry for the first half of the 20th century, in part because seeing self-esteem this way offers many advantages that make good sense. For example, identifying the areas of life that are especially important to a person in terms of his or her sense of self helps professionals, such as clinicians and teachers, better understand those whom they aid. This view also has practical value because once we identify such key areas in someone's life we can help the person improve in those domains. If that is not possible, this approach allows us to help the individual find new areas in which to be successful that are satisfying in regard to identity. In fact, there are several self-esteem programs available that do this type of work (Pope, McHale, & Craighead, 1988).

In short, it is important to recognize the value and usefulness of competence-based definitions of self-esteem. After all, it is difficult to deny that people do better in life when they competently meet its challenges as they arise. Those who lack this essential characteristic are simply at greater risk for a whole host of personal, interpersonal, and sometimes economic problems.

Eventually, however, it became clear even to those who based their work on this way of defining self-esteem that there is a problem with James's definition and the competence approach to self-esteem in general (Crocker & Park, 2004). The problem is that making self-esteem contingent on success also means that failure is very important. An excessive emphasis on success can create self-esteem related difficulties for a person as well as those who are around him or her. For instance, if an individual's self-esteem is too heavily based on being successful in a particular domain of life and if he or she lacks the ability to succeed or suffers an unexpected failure, then that person's identity is easily threatened. Other examples of such behavior may be seen in the lives of those who sacrifice their integrity to pursue success at any cost, such as some well-known political figures, and as seen in various mental disorders, such as anorexia where being too successful at losing weight can result in death.

In general, the vulnerability created by defining self-esteem in terms of success means that such a person must spend considerable psychological resources protecting his or her identity from the threat of failure because it destabilizes one's sense of self. Crocker and Park (2004) investigated this possibility by examining the impact that being rejected had on the self-esteem in a career context. The study measured the self-esteem of promising undergraduate students at a major university who applied to prestigious graduate programs to advance their careers and then measured it again after they had received notices of rejection. All of these participants were very good students, and few people enjoy failure, so the experience was unpleasant. However, the results indicated that only people who strongly tied their identity to being an outstanding student (i.e., someone who is exceptionally smart or unusually promising) suffered a loss in self-esteem. Those who grounded their identities more strongly in other domains of life, such as family, did not.

Although it is easy to see this type of susceptibility in a concrete situation, such as the one previously presented, people whose self-esteem is contingent on success or failure are basically more vulnerable as individuals because success and failure can occur in many spheres of life. In fact, such competence-based self-esteem can be a part of more serious conditions. For instance, most of us know or have known people who are so focused on success that they ignore or even neglect other parts of their lives to pursue it, such as those who sacrifice their physical health or personal relationships to get ahead in terms of careers, money, status, and the like. In addition, this type of self-esteem is often associated with the mental health problems mentioned earlier. In other words, social scientists now realize that competence-based definitions of self-esteem, or those that are contingent on some form of success, are a psychological dead end. In fact, some of the researchers who used this definition, such as Jennifer Crocker and Lora Park previously cited, recommend giving up the search for self-esteem altogether for this very reason.

Defining Self-Esteem as a Form of Worthiness

In the latter part of the 20th century, the field of self-esteem slowly moved toward two other ways of defining it. One such line of work developed because social scientists became interested in measuring self-esteem to research it more thoroughly. Although desirable, measuring competence is difficult to do because it involves such things as identifying specific behaviors to be assessed; establishing norms for what is to be considered poor, average, or good; and then developing tools to make accurate observations or assessments. Around the same time, however, social scientists made considerable progress in measuring things like attitudes, which are much easier to assess because that can be done using something called *self-report* instruments. Anyone who has taken a questionnaire that asks them to rate themselves on a scale from a 1 to a 10 is familiar with this approach.

During this period, the sociologist Morris Rosenberg (1965) developed a simple 10-question self-esteem test of this sort called the Self-Esteem Inventory (SEI). He worked from a sociological view, which, among other things, involves looking at behavior from a larger social perspective rather than one based mainly on individual experience, as was James's approach. Rosenberg defined self-esteem as an attitude or feeling toward oneself concerning his or her worth as a person, which is what I call *worthiness*. In the case of high self-esteem, for instance, he said an individual feels that he or she is "a person of worth" (Rosenberg, 1965, p. 31).

Asking people to rate themselves in this way made measuring self-esteem easier than ever before and the fact that the test only had 10 simple questions meant that it could be given to large groups of people as well as to individuals. One of the most famous studies of this type, which Rosenberg became widely known for, showed that when compared to whites, African American adolescents reported a higher degree of self-esteem (Rosenberg & Simmons, 1971). The point is that the combination of test simplicity and administrative versatility make the instrument highly attractive to social scientists.

During the 1980s, understanding self-esteem in terms of feeling worthwhile as a person became very popular for at least three reasons. One is that defining self-esteem in terms of worth is simply a far more common way of understanding the concept, even though James's and Milton's use of the term clearly involved competence or the ability to stand up for one's oneself. Second, measuring self-esteem is much easier to do when it is defined in terms of feelings of worth rather than behavioral competence. In fact, it has been estimated that at the time nearly one quarter of all research on self-esteem conducted was based on Rosenberg's inventory or something like it (Tafarodi & Swann, 1995), a trend which continues today. Finally, this approach is readily compatible with various social learning and educational theories that were becoming popular at the time, especially those that emphasize the role of such things as positive reinforcement, encouragement, and praise as tools to shape individual identity and social behavior.

In addition to increasing our ability to research self-esteem, there is considerable value in the idea that self-esteem is strongly affected by one's social environment. For example, learning theories are very good at demonstrating how social groups play important roles in providing such things as acceptance in early childhood, developing standards in middle childhood, and striving toward ideals during adulthood. Note that all of these things involve learning about various values, being valued, and different forms of worthiness. Understanding self-esteem as a sense of worth set in a social or environmental context also creates powerful practical possibilities. Chief among them is the idea that if the social environment, including family, education, and peer interaction, affects self-esteem in this way, then we should work hard to avoid creating negative social environments and to foster the development of positive ones. The result of such a focus should be a win–win situation for individuals and for society in general.

For instance, if certain conditions, such as poverty, neglect, or abuse interfere with developing a sense of worth as a person, and they most certainly can, then this approach indicates it should be possible to use the principles of learning and reinforcement to modify negative behavior and to shape prosocial environments in the home, school, workplace, and so on. Also, since we know that positive reinforcement is usually more effective than negative, it should be relatively easy to use the well-known principles of learning and social conditioning to create home, school, and work environments that nurture self-esteem.

In many ways, our culture did just that. During the late 1980s and early 1990s this definition of self-esteem came to dominate the field. At the same time, understanding self-esteem as an attitude or feeling of worth also became very popular with parents, educators, and eventually, politicians. In California, for example, well-intended state senators, such as John Vasconcellos (Smelser, 1989), became convinced self-esteem was something of a psychological magic bullet capable of solving all sorts of personal, interpersonal, and social problems. The idea was that if people felt good about themselves, then they would suffer less depression, have little need for addictions, do better at school, find more value in work than welfare, be better parents, make better citizens, and the like.

As a result, the California self-esteem movement, as it became called, led to a huge increase in the popularity of self-esteem as a concept. Soon the primary goal of many books on parenting and childhood development focused on helping children feel good about themselves at almost any cost. Further, many if not most educational institutions taught teachers to do the same. For example, instead of focusing on developing competence at traditional educational skills, such as math, many educators became trained to make children feel good about their efforts at learning, not its outcomes. Other areas were affected by this type of social engineering as well. In sports or competitive activities, for instance, it became more important to make sure each child was praised for trying, even if his or her performance was poor. Sometimes it even came to the point that instead of learning about working hard, trying one's best, and striving to reach worthy goals, awards were given to every participant just for being present.

The general idea of increasing self-esteem by using positive reinforcement to help children feel good about themselves and to reduce the negative impact of harsh parenting, demeaning educational practices, and other forms of toxic social environments is a good one. However, just as defining self-esteem in terms of competence had negative unintended consequences, so did basing it on worthiness. Consequently, in the mid-1990s several social scientists, some educators, and a number of news media began reporting disturbing news about the self-esteem movement.

Although the possibility was discussed earlier (Mruk, 1995, p. 80), Roy Baumeister and his team (Baumeister, Smart, & Boden, 1996) found that when self-esteem is defined only as a feeling of personal worth, narcissists, antisocial personalities, and some criminals score high on self-esteem tests. In other words,

this way of defining self-esteem includes people who feel very good about themselves even though they often do bad things to others. In addition, psychologists
such as Martin Seligman (1990), a founder of the positive psychology movement,
supported the position that self-esteem is the result of behavior, not a cause of it.
Eventually educators began to notice that although children felt good about their
academic abilities, often they lacked competence at reading, writing, and at doing
basic math. Finally, popular media aimed at the general public began to criticize
the self-esteem movement with provocative titles, such as Charles Krauthammer's
(1990) "Education: Doing Bad and Feeling Good."

Interestingly enough, it is now often reported that although self-esteem among
American college students has risen during the past generation or two, so have
rates of depression, anxiety, and other mental health issues needing treatment
at colleges and universities, as indicated by dramatic increases in the use of their
counseling centers and services. In sum, although being accepted or valued by
others can make a person feel worthy, and while feeling good about oneself is important for well-being, defining self-esteem this way leads to another set of fatal
problems that are made worse by the fact that this type of definition is the one that
is most commonly used. In fact, the problem with self-esteem became so great
that the term was scaled back in many psychological and educational textbooks
and is sometimes no longer even mentioned. In a word, the concept of self-esteem
came close to being abandoned in what I have described as a crisis of self-esteem
(Mruk, 2013a).

Defining Self-Esteem as a Relationship between Competence and Worthiness

The results of understanding self-esteem either as a sense of competence or worthiness alone appear to be different types of conceptual fatal flaws. Even further,
these limitations are so severe that they may encourage some people to reject the
importance of the concept of self-esteem in general. If these two ways of defining
self-esteem were the only ones available, I would not be interested in writing
another book on it. However, the business of science, including social science,
requires using the scientific method, and this approach to knowledge is a self-
correcting one. Like many other crises in science, the result of the one concerning
the classical concept of self-esteem turns out to be a serendipitous event because
pointing out an important weakness can lead to significant improvements.

For one thing, social scientists began doing work on self-esteem in other cultures,
including Japan, China, and more. In fact, one global study of self-esteem found
that it is important to people in some 53 countries around the world (Schmitt &
Allik, 2005). Other social scientists noted that high self-esteem correlates with
such things as happiness and well-being while low self-esteem is associated with
many types of personal and interpersonal problems. Finally, knowing about the
flaws in defining self-esteem in terms of only one factor, namely, competence or
worthiness, forced social scientists to reexamine the concept in a more detailed

fashion. A very important result of this process was a new focus on a third major definition of self-esteem, one that addresses the shortcomings found in the others.

Abraham Maslow (1954/1970) talked about both competence and worthiness in relation to self-esteem in 1954. But Nathaniel Branden (1969) seems to have first fully articulated the relationship between these two factors a decade later when he said,

> Self-esteem has two interrelated aspects: it entails a sense of personal efficacy and a sense of personal worth. It is the integrated sum of self-confidence and self-respect. It is the conviction that one is *competent* to live and *worthy* of living. (p. 110)

Today, those who research self-esteem from this point of view simply call it the *two-factor* approach (Tafarodi & Swann, 1995) for obvious reasons.

Let us take a moment to unfold this way of seeing self-esteem by looking at both of its components of competence and worthiness as well as the nature of the relationship between them. Two aspects of competence are important for self-esteem. One is what social scientists often call *self-efficacy*, which involves believing in one's skills or abilities. Sometimes people confuse this concept with self-esteem, but it is a mistake to take beliefs for realities. Thus, self-efficacy is only one part of competence. The other one is actually having the skills or abilities necessary to successfully do something.

Worthiness is tied to that which is admired, honored, cherished, or valued for its inherent qualities. Although there is debate as to whether there are universal values that reflect basic human nature, considerable cross-cultural research on self-esteem and positive psychology-based research on virtue suggest that certain types of values are respected by most people, in most cultures, and throughout most of human history (Peterson & Seligman, 2004; Sedikides, Gaertner, & Cai, 2015). They include things like courage, integrity, honor, and actualization, all of which are related to the concept of authenticity and give us good reason to use that word to mean self-esteem that is real, high, and healthy.

The relationship between competence and worthiness may be thought of as a function, which means that they work together to produce an outcome or product, in this case self-esteem. In other words, self-esteem is not just being able to do various things effectively. Nor is it simply a matter of feeling good about oneself as a person. Instead, when defined this way, authentic self-esteem always requires a person to demonstrate competence but in ways that are worthy of a mature and fully functioning or healthy human being. In a word, authentic self-esteem must be earned.

This definition of self-esteem eliminates some of the problems created by the others. For example, people who demonstrate competence without doing so in worthwhile ways could not be seen as having authentic self-esteem because their actions are unbalanced. Thus, schoolyard or workplace bullies and antisocial individuals who are very competent at taking advantage of people in physical, emotional, or social ways would not be considered to have authentic self-esteem according to the two-factor definition. The reason, of course, is that their behavior does not include the other factor, namely, actions that demonstrate the person is worthy or capable of doing that which is just and right, as Milton might say it. Quite literally, then, authentic self-esteem cannot involve feeling good while doing bad to oneself or to others according to this two-factor definition.

Similarly, feeling good about oneself without doing something that actually warrants such an evaluation or reaction would also not count as authentic self-esteem according to the two-factor definition. For instance, narcissists feel extremely good about themselves but often treat others badly, which is hardly worthy of a fully functioning adult. Research also shows that some criminals feel quite good about themselves most of the time and that they may even test high on self-esteem instruments because of that (Baumeister, Smart, & Boden, 1996). Clearly, such people or scores would not be consistent with Milton's concept of doing that which is just and right, which is at the heart of the original definition of self-esteem. In short, competence without worthiness cannot create authentic self-esteem, and a sense of worth without competence is just as inadequate. According to the two-factor definition, both must be present for self-esteem to occur because the relationship is such that each factor balances the other, a condition that avoids the problems found in the other definitions.

Unfortunately, there are limits to every definition. Although the two-factor approach does not suffer the problems found in the other two ways of defining self-esteem because of the reciprocal nature of the relationship between them, it is not without difficulties. Among them is that working with a complex definition is much more challenging than using a simple one. People usually take longer to understand more sophisticated definitions; they are not convenient, and they do not sell well, especially to popular media. In addition, complex terms often slow down discussions even when people are interested in them. And, most of all, researching two factors working together is much more difficult than focusing on only one or the other. Consequently, it is not surprising that this approach is not as well recognized even though it is the only path to authentic self-esteem.

Fortunately, research support for this way of defining self-esteem reached a critical mass that makes it necessary for people to consider the two-factor view when talking about self-esteem if they wish to be thorough. For instance, Romin Tafarodi and his colleagues (Tafarodi & Vu, 1997) offer a powerful analogy that helps understand the approach, how it works, and why it is so effective. Competence and worthiness, or *self-competence* and *self-liking*, as they described it, are compared to lines on a piece of paper. By themselves, two lines form nothing in particular. However, when one is seen in terms of length and the other is identified as width, they make something distinct, new, and meaningful, namely, the well-recognized space called a rectangle.

I prefer to sharpen the analogy by taking it one step further in my work on self-esteem. According to the two-factor approach, competence and worthiness act as partners in creating self-esteem, which implies a certain type of relationship. Not only must both "lines" be present to have authentic self-esteem, but they also play equally significant roles in developing and maintaining healthy or authentic self-esteem. In other words, a deficiency in one factor also distorts the other. There is only one type of rectangle that reflects a relationship where both sets of lines are equal or balanced like this and that is a square. Another advantage of using this analogy is that it lends itself to visual representation, as we shall encounter shortly, that many find helpful in understanding not only authentic self-esteem but inauthentic forms of it as well.

The first question in representing the two factors as a square is which one will stand as height and which one is to represent width? I always identify worthiness as height because it ranges from extremely low states, such as those that might be seen in suicidal depression, to medium ones, which is much more average or common, all the way to a very positive sense of one's worth as seen in high self-esteem. Feelings also happen to work this way as they can range from low to high or from negative to positive, with medium levels in between the extremes. There is also a certain value or moral dimension ranging from low to high that supports this placement. For example, Milton could have taken the lower road to handling the challenge to his integrity by denying it or by feeling sorry for himself. Instead, he took the higher and more difficult but worthy alternative of rising to the challenge and risk facing it.

Competence is represented by the horizontal line for good reasons as well. For instance, competence involves abilities, skills, and performances, many of which can be observed or measured on a scale based on a continuum of possibilities that range from one end to the other. Social scientists call this way of describing things a *distribution*, and it usually is depicted as a horizontal line with the norm or average in the middle and very poor or exceptionally good at the extremes. In fact, we measure many types of behavior and characteristics in this fashion, such as height, weight, athletic ability, IQ, and so forth.

This approach to representing the two factors even makes it possible to attribute numerical ratings to each factor. For example, both of them could be seen as ranging from a +10 to a −10. Finally, the two factors and the relationship between them can be represented visually as in Figure 1.1.

This illustration captures several important dimensions of self-esteem that are worth noticing. For instance, the intersection of the two factors at the zero point in the middle demonstrates the nature of the relationship between the two factors. Thus, instead of representing nothing, this point shows how competence and worthiness are equal partners that operate together to create the larger existential space of the square called self-esteem by psychologists and others.

Next, it is not accidental that competence and worthiness interact in a way that results in four basic types of self-esteem. Authentic self-esteem, which is created only when competence and worthiness balance each other in a positive or healthy way, is found in the upper right-hand quadrant (B) where both factors are high and positive. The opposite quadrant (C) is balanced too, but in a negative direction, so it represents low self-esteem, and the corresponding coordinates are both low. Like other negative states, low self-esteem often creates conditions of greater vulnerability, in this case to anything that might threaten identity. It is even possible to identify very high and extremely low self-esteem by the coordinates of +10

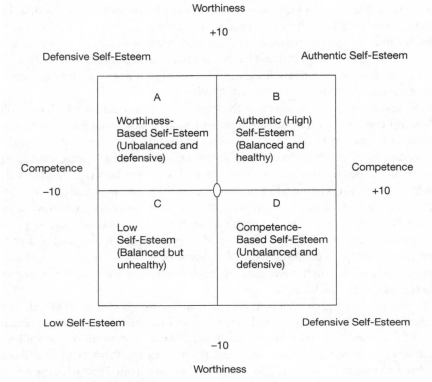

Figure 1.1   Basic Types of Self-Esteem
Source: Modified from Mruk, C. (2013). *Self-Esteem and positive psychology: Research, theory, and practice* (4th ed.). New York, Springer Publishing Company.

and +10 and −10 and −10 and −10, respectively, if one is interested in a more quantitative model of self-esteem.

However, the other two quadrants are clearly unbalanced because in each of them one factor is positive while the other is in some way deficient or negative. This pattern is extremely important because it indicates that the relationship between the two factors is unstable, conflicted, or perhaps even fragile. This condition, we shall see in chapter 2, contributes to problems with self-regulation, such as psychological instability, defensiveness, and destructiveness toward self or others. In the upper left quadrant (A), for example, we see a positive sense of worth that is not accompanied by a corresponding degree of competence. Such *worthiness-based self-esteem*, as I call it, occurs when an individual feels good about himself or herself but does little to merit such an opinion. We find the opposite arrangement in the lower right quadrant (D) where a person may be very competent, but either feels empty despite being successful or might even feel good as a result of doing bad things, either of which reflects an absence of worth. *Competence-based self-esteem* must, therefore, also be understood as a form of inauthentic or unhealthy self-esteem.

SELF-ESTEEM TYPES, LEVELS, AND PROBLEMS

Understanding self-esteem as a relationship between competence and worthiness has several advantages not found in other approaches. However, before describing them it is first necessary to return to an important if not crucial matter: The zero point on the grid represents the intersection of competence and worthiness and how they work together. In no way does that point mean an absence of self-esteem. Rather, each axis of the diagram represents a continuum of behavior, and zero represents their middle or average range. It is true that some people behave in ways that reflect very high levels of worthiness, such as those who make serious sacrifices for others. Similarly, other people demonstrate a total lack of worthiness, such as ruthless dictators. But most people are somewhere in the middle. Competence works the same way: Some people are very good at a given skill, such as athletics or mathematics, others are very poor at it, and most are somewhere in the middle, which would be the zero point in the diagram.

The combination of a modest degree of competence and worthiness is called *medium self-esteem* by some researchers. It occurs in the same quadrant as authentic self-esteem because all healthy self-esteem, even modest degrees of it, is based on having some degree of both factors. As just indicated, it is also important to realize that each type of self-esteem has two levels: One is more moderate or fairly common while the other is more unusual or extreme. In each case, these two levels reflect different degrees of the characteristics associated with the relationship between competence and worthiness in a given quadrant or type of self-esteem.

For example, authentic self-esteem involves a high degree of competence and worthiness, while medium self-esteem consists of less of each factor. Similarly, one level of low self-esteem is moderate, which means that such an individual may be quite functional but not happy. However, someone at the more extreme level is likely to suffer depression or other types of mental health problems associated with low self-esteem. Worthiness-based self-esteem might involve moodiness and feelings of insecurity, while narcissists would be found in the more extreme or outer section of the same quadrant. Moderate competence-based self-esteem problems are likely to be seen in overachievers, but antisocial personalities would be on the more extreme end of the quadrant characterized by high competence but low worthiness.

Low Self-Esteem

Because low self-esteem involves a deficiency of both factors, it is represented in the lower left quadrant (C). In general, most people have heard quite a bit about how very low self-esteem is associated with a number of problems including poor performance, the inability to handle stress, anxiety, depression, substance abuse, negative relationships, self-defeating behavior, and even suicide. People with very low levels of self-esteem are also at risk for a number of interpersonal problems. One reason for this vulnerability, of course, is that having little self-esteem means having less in the way of emotional and mental resources for handling the challenges of living. Being less able to handle stress, in turn, makes people more susceptible to all sorts of negative personal and interpersonal possibilities. As a clinician, of course, I have known many people with severely low levels of self-esteem.

However, most people don't realize that the picture is rather different for those with mildly to moderately low self-esteem. This level can be represented as being nearer the upper portion of the same quadrant. To be sure, low self-esteem is not a pleasant state in which to be personally or interpersonally, but this level of low self-esteem is not clinically significant. Contrary to popular opinion, for instance, most people with this moderate level of low self-esteem do not walk around like the psychologically wounded. In other words, they do not hate themselves. Indeed, they don't even feel terribly bad about themselves. Instead, many people with mild levels of low self-esteem simply tend to focus on protecting this valuable resource rather than expanding it. To them, protecting the self and maintaining a stable sense of identity is much more important than risking the self even if that is the way to grow or expand identity and well-being (Tice, 1993).

Mildly low self-esteem, for example, is often accompanied by something called *self-handicapping*, which is a way of regulating behavior so that self-esteem is protected. Such individuals are very interested in the opportunity to be more successful or more valued when such times come along in life. However, instead of focusing on the positive opportunities that come with taking the risks necessary for good things to actually occur, they focus on the potentially negative ones, such as the possibility of failure or embarrassment. These outcomes would result in a loss of self-esteem, so instead of making a full commitment to doing what is necessary to support personal or interpersonal growth, they hold back or psychologically hedge their bets.

The logic of this strategy runs something like this: "If I prepare myself for failure, then I won't feel as bad as if I really tried hard and failed. If I don't try my best, then I can always say to myself and others that maybe the next time I'll do better." Or the reasoning might go, "I want to get closer to this person, but I don't want to feel rejected. Therefore, I'll give him or her a hint about my interest and maybe he or she will respond. If not, I can blame it on the fact that I didn't really express my intent well or that the other person failed to see it at the time." Psychologists also call this type of thinking *rationalization*, and its purpose is to defend the self.

Unfortunately, there is a self-fulfilling dimension to such reasoning. We first saw this aspect of low self-esteem when describing M in the introduction to the chapter. In her case, for example, it was suggested that the self-handicapping strategy she used to avoid threats to her self-esteem helped keep her from succeeding in areas that were important to her. Similarly, depending on the approval of others at the expense of one's worthiness can also become a vicious self-esteem cycle. In short, while a protective personal and interpersonal focus does not result in experiencing a meaningful degree of well-being, such as people with even medium self-esteem might have, mild or moderately low self-esteem does not necessarily mean a bad life, just a less satisfying one.

Unbalanced or Defensive Self-Esteem

The diagram indicates that there are two forms of self-esteem distinguished by the fact that they lack balance. Worthiness-based self-esteem is found in the upper left quadrant (A) of the diagram where it is possible to feel good about oneself but not necessarily in ways that merit such an opinion, which makes the feeling hollow or inauthentic. In other words, these individuals have an unwarranted or inflated positive image of themselves that results in its own set of individual and social problems. In particular, the lack of competence concerning their ability to effectively deal with life's challenges or to handle stress creates a state of defensiveness lest the individual be unmasked in this way.

Typically, worthiness-based self-esteem is expressed in two ways. First, some people who base most of their self-esteem on feeling worthy try to obtain it from others. That is, they tend to rely on various external forms of acceptance, approval, or praise to help feel worthwhile as a person. Although most people desire such social rewards, those with worthiness-based self-esteem need it more and often find themselves giving up what they want to please others too often, trying too hard to impress people in general, being overly worried about whether others like them, and/or having difficulties being alone.

Second, the lack of competence associated with this condition means that such people have little to fall back on when facing challenges. Accordingly, they are especially sensitive to interpersonal forms of stress, such as criticism, rejection, disapproval, or embarrassment. If desperate enough, such individuals may even try to bolster their sense of worth through negative means, such as putting others down, exaggerating their own importance, overstating their accomplishments (bragging), and the like.

Although it is easy to dismiss children who behave in this fashion by seeing them as spoiled, the adult version is much less pleasant. Sometimes they are just an obnoxious coworker who people do not want on their team or a self-centered relative who is tolerated only as long as necessary. However, in more extreme or clinical levels, the lack of balance found in worthiness-based self-esteem rises to the level of a narcissistic personality disorder. For instance, the sense of entitlement or exaggerated self-importance indicative of these conditions might be manifestations of such a self-esteem issue. In the most severe situations, such an individual might even resort to violence to defend against threats to a fragile sense of self. The inability to handle rejection seen in an abandoned spouse who stalks his or her former partner might be a case in point.

The other form of unbalanced or defensive self-esteem is found in the lower right quadrant (D). This combination of the two factors affecting self-esteem involves a real degree of ability but is also characterized by a low sense of worthiness to balance the quality of one's actions. This situation results in an individual who is problematically dependent upon success. Of course, it is important to realize that there are many ways to be successful. Some are more individually oriented, such as academic, athletic, career, and financial success. Others are more social or interpersonal, such as being admired or having higher social status. Once again, mild levels of this defensive type of self-esteem certainly detract from well-being but they do not necessarily damage a life or relationships. More severe levels often do cause such destruction, and they are also connected to clinically significant as well as unhealthy modes of personal and interpersonal behavior including anger, aggression, bullying, and the like.

A classic example of a mild variety of this type of self-esteem in action is the overachiever who strives toward success in ways that detract from other parts of his or her life. For example, as an academic, I have often seen students who focus far too much on having a very high grade point average at the expense of their physical well-being or social development. Such *A-itis*, as it is euphemistically called, sometimes results in the individual suffering a sense of loneliness or desperation that ends badly. If they are more fortunate, they make it to the counseling center instead. Some of the students in Crocker and Park's research mentioned earlier might be included in this group.

What differentiates such a person from someone with a healthier pursuit of success is that he or she needs it to maintain a stable sense of self. This type of individual's low sense of worth means that there is no alternative route to feeling good as a person other than to be first, to have the most, to be the best, and so on in the domains of life that are tied to his or her identity. As long as success occurs in these areas of life, the individual appears to be in pretty good psychological shape and may even rise to the top in his or her field. The difficulty is that their success cannot be savored for long because their feelings of worthlessness persist. Instead of enjoying their lives, people like this are typically compelled to prove themselves on an endless obstacle course of success, sometimes at a considerable cost to relationships, health, and well-being—all to avoid fully experiencing or dealing with a lack of worth.

Since failure is the other side of success when it is used for self-esteem, the threat of personal or interpersonal failure makes such people very vulnerable in life because without success, there is little left to buffer or to sustain their identities. In the more clinically severe cases at the outer level of this type, competence-based self-esteem can even result in antisocial behavior conducted to obtain success or to defend one's self in the case of failure. Those who possess a high degree of competence but who have little sense of a conscience to balance such ability also put others at risk in their relationships. In the most extreme cases, such a person may destroy whole groups of people to demonstrate his or her superiority, such as in the case of a ruthless dictator.

The bottom line is that while people with low self-esteem must expend energy regulating behavior in self-protective ways, at least the two factors are balanced, which means that their self-esteem is stable. While those with either level of low self-esteem are often harder on themselves than others, their pain is also experienced more directly, which may help them seek out help more readily. However, the presence of one positive factor and one negative factor makes self-images less stable, sometimes even fragile. In addition, having one foot on the positive side is a complicating factor because, while it is good to function well or to feel good in certain areas of life, focusing on that part of reality makes it easier to deny problems in other areas. Consequently, competence or worthiness-based defensive self-esteem is characterized by more self-deception and a greater tendency to act out against others rather than to act within, as in depression. This combination, of course, makes change more difficult.

In more complicated cases, the underlying lack of balance between the two factors can even be expressed by a tendency to psychologically and behaviorally slide back and forth between the two unbalanced quadrants. This type of self-esteem problem is characterized by high degrees of fragility and, therefore, excessive defensiveness, sometimes even in the face of only minor setbacks or well-intended criticism. This self-esteem dynamic is often seen in borderline, bipolar, narcissistic, and antisocial personality disorders that may strike out when challenged by others.

High Self-Esteem (Medium and Authentic)

Like the other types, high self-esteem also occurs at two levels. As described earlier, medium self-esteem can be thought of as being average or normal self-esteem. Though often ignored in discussions of self-esteem, there are two good reasons to focus on medium self-esteem. First, and as previously mentioned, it is difficult to deny that this level is where most of us tend to be in life. For instance, self-esteem tests are designed to pick up variations from the norm. To do that, it is necessary to know what the average level is. Only then can we identify less common forms of it, such as low, defensive, or authentic self-esteem.

Second, having normal, average, typical, or medium self-esteem is usually necessary to reach a higher, which is to say, authentic, level. The fact of the matter is that most of us demonstrate some degree of competence at dealing with the challenges of living, and most people usually try their best to live their lives in a worthwhile fashion. In contrast to low or defensive self-esteem, this configuration of competence and worthiness means that people with medium self-esteem find personal and interpersonal growth as important as protecting or maintaining the self. The upshot is, of course, that most people are very much interested in reaching higher or more satisfying degrees of well-being, even if it means risking failure more often. This medium level of high self-esteem can be seen in the lower portion of the upper right-hand quadrant (B) created by the intersection of a positive but modest degree of competence and worthiness as seen in Figure 1.2.

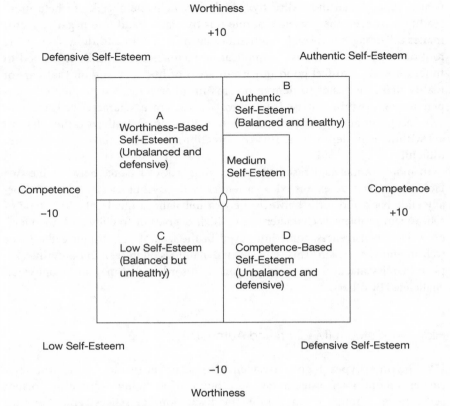

Figure 1.2 Medium Self-Esteem
Source: Modified from Mruk, C. (2013). *Self-Esteem and positive psychology: Research, theory, and practice* (4th ed.). New York, Springer Publishing Company.

Authentic (Balanced and High) Self-Esteem

So far, we have discussed defining self-esteem, become aware of the limits of basing definitions on only one factor, and have seen that there are several types of self-esteem, each of which has two levels. That work prepares us to examine the characteristics of the highest type and level: authentic self-esteem. First, because authentic self-esteem requires high levels of competence and worthiness, it is only found in the upper part of that quadrant (area B). Second, we have also seen that the other two ways of defining self-esteem also talk about high self-esteem, some of which is healthy and some of which is very unhealthy. Thus, it is necessary to specify how authentic self-esteem is different.

The distinguishing feature of authentic self-esteem is that it is based on a positive relationship between competence and worthiness like medium self-esteem, only much more so. The difference between the two levels is found in the degree to which self-esteem is involved in the process of actualizing. Whether it involves reaching personal or interpersonal goals or maintaining a sense of individual or relational worth, those with authentic self-esteem are better able to actualize possibilities. In other words, not only do they tolerate stress better, but they also regularly take the risks necessary to grow, develop, and expand personally and interpersonally to optimize well-being.

This real self-esteem has gone by several names over time, including high self-esteem, healthy self-esteem, positive self-esteem, and authentic self-esteem, all of which can generate some confusion. Using operational definitions to deal with the problem of ambiguity caused by sloppy definitions once again, I prefer the term *authentic self-esteem* for several reasons. The most obvious is that the word authentic means genuine, which is in itself helpful because it reminds us that although someone may score high on a self-esteem test, it does not necessarily mean he or she possesses healthy self-esteem.

Further, the word *authentic* also helps us to be mindful that there are lesser or inauthentic forms of self-esteem, such as the two varieties of defensive self-esteem previously described. Next, some researchers have done exciting empirical work connecting this type and level of self-esteem with the quality of authenticity and well-being in general. This connection is especially important because authenticity also is a well-established concept in existential philosophy and humanistic psychology that involves several healthy human characteristics related to self-esteem. They include higher degrees of self-awareness, a greater sense of self-acceptance, and increased genuineness with others, all of which are helpful in making good (healthy or growth oriented) life choices. Finally, the field of positive psychology indicates that authenticity is among the basic human virtues associated with well-being.

Michael Kernis (2003) has probably done more scientific research than anyone else on the connections between authenticity, self-esteem, and well-being as part of his work on what he calls *optimal* self-esteem. Basically, he found that this highest form of self-esteem is characterized by four main qualities: (a) being secure enough to perceive and admit to personal faults and limitations; (b) being consistent in one's behavior toward self and others in that one's actions are characterized by a low level of defensiveness; (c) being genuine because such individuals do not require continual validation of worthiness from others or endless successes to sustain a sense of identity; and (d) being stable, which comes from being balanced enough to be open to taking the risks necessary to grow and expand the self more than focusing on self-protection. One way to think about an authentic sense of self-esteem, then, is to imagine a person who is generally secure, usually consistent, frequently genuine, and reliably stable in the way he or she deals with self, others, and the challenges of living. Who would shun such positive qualities and their implications for well-being?

Individual Self-Esteem

It is helpful to understand at least one more thing about types and levels of self-esteem. Just as with many other things in life, such as personality characteristics, very few people are pure types. After all, even those with authentic self-esteem cannot be authentic all of the time. Thus, when thinking about any particular person's self-esteem, it is important to realize that there is plenty of individual variability to consider. Why that occurs will be discussed in chapter 3 while examining the development of self-esteem. For now, this dimension of self-esteem can be illustrated by plotting M's self-esteem on the diagram as shown in Figure 1.3.

M's profile might take this form because it depicts a genuine problem with moderately low self-esteem as competence and worthiness are lacking in that quadrant, something that is very consistent with the diagnosis of depression along with some anxiety. However, it is important to note that she also possesses a meaningful degree of medium self-esteem, which means that it should be possible to help her move toward more authentic self-esteem at some point in the treatment process.

Finally, although most books on self-esteem focus only on the possibility of increasing it, the fact of the matter is that if self-esteem can change in a positive way, it only stands to reason that we can lose self-esteem in life as well. I explore these two themes throughout the book, but for now it is important to emphasize how competence and worthiness work together to create authentic self-esteem.

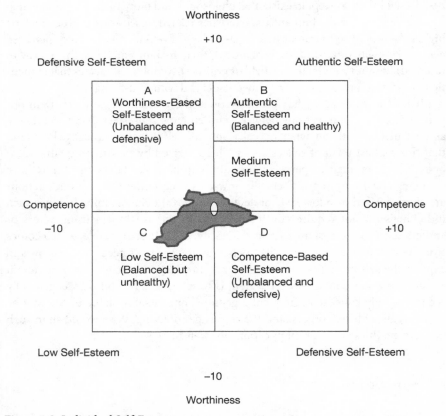

Figure 1.3 Individual Self-Esteem
Source: Modified from Mruk, C. (2013). *Self-Esteem and positive psychology: Research, theory, and practice* (4th ed.). New York, Springer Publishing Company.

Since many people find something called *thought activities* helpful in understanding a concept or in applying it to everyday life, I will offer 10 of them in this book.

The first one begins with Box 1.1a, which is designed to help make the dynamic relationship between the two factors clearer both conceptually and experientially. Initially, the illustration simply involves taking M through the exercise to show how it works. Next to be offered is Box 1.1b, which is a blank form for those who

---

Box 1.1a

THOUGHT ACTIVITY: APPRECIATING THE TWO COMPONENTS
OF AUTHENTIC SELF-ESTEEM

1. Describe an experience or situation that involved feeling worthwhile as a person.
   M's example: "I was at work today and saw one of my colleagues struggling with carrying things to another area in the building. So I stopped what I was doing to help him out."

2. Describe an experience or situation in which you were competent at something.
   M's example: "I had been working on this problem for an hour earlier today and then found a solution everyone else missed that seems to work just right."

3. Describe an experience or situation in which you were competent at doing something worthy.
   M's example: "I made a mistake at work today. I hate making mistakes and admitting them is even worse. So I was tempted to hide it by blaming someone else or by pretending I didn't realize I made an error. I know I could have gotten away with it too. But instead of taking the easy way out, I stood up to the situation, admitted my error, and took responsibility for fixing it."

4. Summarize what these experiences show you about authentic self-esteem.
   M's example: "There are many things I can see about the two factors of self-esteem here and how they are connected to each other. One is that doing something good for another person when they need it makes me feel worthwhile as a person. Maybe I should do that more often. I can also see how competence feels good: At least it sure felt empowering when I solved the problem that challenge presented! Finally, I learned that competence and worthiness are related to self-esteem just as Milton said. It wasn't easy to admit that mistake in front of others. But I knew lying or sneaking was not the best answer and at least I had the integrity to do the right thing, even though it wasn't fun. It is clear that authentically facing even such a small challenge of living feels better than what I was tempted to do."

Box 1.1b

THOUGHT ACTIVITY: APPRECIATING THE TWO COMPONENTS OF AUTHENTIC
SELF-ESTEEM

1. Describe an experience or situation that involved feeling worthwhile
   as a person.

   _____

   _____

   _____

   _____

2. Describe an experience or situation in which you were competent at
   something.

   _____

   _____

   _____

   _____

3. Describe an experience or situation in which you were competent at doing
   something worthy.

   _____

   _____

   _____

   _____

4. Summarize what these experiences show you about authentic self-esteem.

   _____

   _____

   _____

   _____

Source: Modified from Mruk, C. (2013). *Self-Esteem and positive psychology: Research, theory, and practice* (4th ed.). New York, Springer Publishing Company.

wish to try the activity out. The activity focuses on exploring competence, worthiness, and how they can work together to form authentic self-esteem.

Note that it is not necessary to look for big—that is, dramatic or significant—examples. These are important self-esteem moments, and we will explore them in chapter 3. But there are many more small moments in life than large ones, and, because they can add up, everyday experiences may be even more valuable over time. Some people find value in keeping an ongoing self-esteem journal on paper or in a computer file because they tend to prefer more active forms of learning. There is good research supporting the value of doing this type of work on a regular basis, so it may be worth trying (Duckworth, Steen, & Seligman, 2005; Mruk, 2013a).

By now it should be clear that the two-factor approach to defining self-esteem is considerably superior to unidimensional understandings based on either competence or worthiness alone. In addition to avoiding the pitfalls to which other approaches are prone, another benefit this way of thinking about self-esteem offers is that it shows the dynamic character of self-esteem. This dimension of self-esteem, for example, reveals the important fact that there are four basic types of self-esteem to keep in mind. Since each type has two levels, the two-factor approach also helps account for all the different ways in which self-esteem may be expressed by people and their problems. Finally, this dynamic characteristic also is very useful in helping to make connections between self-esteem and behavior, which is the aim of chapter 2.

The Importance of Self-Esteem

Positive Self-Regulation and Control

Since people have been studying self-esteem for more than a century, it is not surprising that there are a good number of theories about what self-esteem does and why it is so important. Although I detail many of them elsewhere (Mruk, 2013a), they can be grouped into three general types: those that focus on the maintenance of the self or self-protection, the ability to control one's experience and behavior or self-control, and growth or self-expansion. While they all take into account the importance of self-esteem in relation to personal and interpersonal well-being, or the lack of it, each approach makes a unique contribution to our understanding of self-esteem because each one emphasizes different dimensions of it.

THREE MAJOR THEORIES OF SELF-ESTEEM

Maintenance (Consistency) Theories

The first general perspective on self-esteem to emerge may be described as maintenance theories because they all focus on the formation of the self, the importance of personal identity, and the way self-esteem protects both. The theory that William James offered is of this type. However, Susan Harter (1999) developed a far more elaborate and modern version. Indeed, she may have written the most comprehensive scholarly work on the development of self-esteem in childhood and adolescence to date.

The general view is based on several principles. One is that human development truly is a psychosocial process, which means that mental and social processes work together to create something—in this case, a self. It begins in terms of the relationships we have with others starting in infancy and how we respond to them as we develop. This process is characterized by experimenting with various social roles associated with each phase of life, which makes development a social as well as a psychological journey. The second principle involves being exposed to various domains of life at each major stage of the life cycle. In childhood, for instance, school offers a number of challenges with which we must deal in the form of increasingly sophisticated academic, physical, and social opportunities. At each step of the way, the developing person experiences positive and negative feedback from others, has pleasant and unpleasant personal experiences, and notices that some areas of life are more interesting than others. These two principles work together to create basic patterns of experience that become the foundations for personal identity and a sense of self. The third principle involves securing these gains by helping the self maintain a degree of stability that allows the individual to achieve a sense of personal identity that is relatively steady over time, which is why this approach is also referred to as consistency theories of self-esteem.

Developmental psychology indicates that around age 18 months or so young children begin to develop a sense of self, although identity comes later. For example, the classic rouge experiment involves coloring an area on a child's face with rouge and then placing him or her in front of a mirror. Before 18 months infants will simply look at their images as though they are seeing another child. After that age, however, they begin to focus on the rouge by touching it while looking at the mirror, indicating that they understand it is on *their* faces, not on another face or an image. Over time, this sense of self in the world acts as a focal point for organizing personal and interpersonal experiences. Those that occur in the more important spheres of life—namely, relationships with significant others and the domains of activity that are important developmentally at the time—become the building blocks of identity.

The self helps individuals make sense of the world and identity allows one to have a familiar place in it. Today cognitive developmental psychologists even tie the formation of these basic psychological patterns to the process of neural sculpting, which concerns the ability of the brain to recognize, form, and use patterns of perception, behavior, and understanding. Once the neural networks and patterns concerning the self and world begin to solidify, they need something to hold them together so that a stable sense of identity may form. That something is self-esteem.

Consequently, theorists, researchers, and clinicians who study and help people based on the maintenance approach emphasize the way self-esteem acts to stabilize or maintain the self and identity: It does so by shielding or buffering people from the threats that come with failure, disappointment, rejection, loss, and the like. In this sense, self-esteem may be seen as a psychological shield that protects the individual from the well-known slings and arrows of life, both small and large. The stronger one's shield happens to be, the better he or she can forge ahead in life and strive toward his or her goals despite the challenges that are sure to accompany them. Conversely, the weaker a person's shield is, the more vulnerable to personal and interpersonal threats that individual becomes. In other words, the quality of one's self-esteem plays a very important role in determining his or her level of well-being.

A simple way of experiencing something of the way that maintenance theories work is to identify and list the social roles and domains of life that matter the most to an individual because they are most likely to be the foundations for one's identity. For example, I once had a particularly diligent student who did a class project on self-esteem by trying to map out all of the beliefs, assumptions, roles, and domains that characterized his own *self-theory*, as it is called by contemporary psychologists. The individual then noted how self-esteem worked to reinforce and protect or buffer these core patterns when life became difficult.

Seymour Epstein (1979) actually studied how self-esteem and the self work together in terms of identity when he asked a group of subjects to track the ups and downs of their feelings about themselves over an extended period of time. He found that self-esteem and identity varied with success and failure in the areas of life that were personally significant, just as James and Harter proposed. Moreover, Epstein found the same pattern in regard to interpersonal life. For example, being affirmed or rejected by significant others had the same type of positive or negative impact on self-esteem. In general, positive personal and interpersonal experiences increased self-esteem and negative ones decreased it. However, those with reasonably good self-esteem to begin with suffered less distress and recovered more quickly.

Control Theories

Other theories of self-esteem, especially those favored by evolutionary social scientists, focus more on self-control than maintenance or protection. For example, the sociometer theory (Leary, 2004) proposes that self-esteem evolved to help us survive as a species. This idea is based on two important observations. One is that, as a species, human beings are extremely dependent on other people. According to evolutionary thinking, human beings emerged from primates who existed in small groups in which members helped each other to survive much as a family would. Some types of monkeys, for example, even have elaborate social orders in which it is important to establish and maintain their individual relationships with other monkeys. Early human beings, of course, depended on each other throughout their entire lives because they usually had to work together to find food, raise children, and get through difficult times. This situation gave rise to communal rather than individual values, a practice that dominated most of human history.

Although it may look as though we are independent today, imagine what would happen if people stopped interacting with each other in an organized, interdependent way. Cars would break down, homes would go without heat or water, and most of us would have little food. In general, modern society would collapse and many, if not most, of us would die rather quickly, especially the young and the old. The point is that regulating social behavior is very important for human beings, so much so that some evolutionary researchers advance the idea that self-esteem developed as a way of helping people to control behavior in relation to the group to enhance everyone's chances of survival.

According to sociometer theory, for instance, self-esteem evolved as a type of meter or gauge to help govern behavior by monitoring it, especially in social situations. In other words, when someone does something that threatens the group, such as acting too selfishly or too aggressively in relation to others, an internal monitor or *sociometer*, as it is called, dips downward, which diminishes the individual's sense of worth or value. This negative feeling, in turn, is a signal that reminds the person to examine his or her behavior and to make appropriate adjustments to avoid disrupting social interaction or even banishment, which was likely to be deadly in those early days. When the individual makes an adaptive response, the sociometer registers it, the gauge returns to the "normal" position, and the person feels better, which is also reinforcing for future behavior.

Since evolution is concerned with the survival of the species in the future as well as the present, the sociometer is also very responsive to prosocial behavior. In this case, when the individual does something to increase the group's chances of survival, such as helping someone who needs it, discovering new resources, creating useful inventions, leading in effective ways, and so on, he or she receives positive social feedback. This reward, in turn, moves the gauge up, thereby encouraging more behavior of a similar adaptive type.

This self-monitoring system is based on various neurological and perceptual processes in the brain called *modules*. When seen this way, the evolution of self-esteem also helps its proponents understand important behavioral and social problems with self-control. For instance, one person's self-esteem may become stuck on "low," which tends to make life more difficult for him or her personally or interpersonally. Another's self-esteem may become unreasonably high, which might result in a lack of self-control that causes disruption for those around him or her. And yet someone else's sociometer may swing back and forth like a broken gauge, which is even more problematic. Some of these possibilities, of course, can occur in relatively mild ways, such as those that happen on a bad day. Others may develop into one of the more problematic types of self-esteem described in chapter 1. A relative few may even manifest themselves in the types of mental disorders associated with low or defensive self-esteem, such as depression, narcissism, and bipolar disorder, respectively, in the three instances just described.

A more existential version of control theory is found in terror management theory (Pyszczynski, Greenberg, & Goldberg, 2003). In this case, self-esteem is seen as an adaptive response to living with the awful knowledge that one is going to die, something that is made worse by the fact that it could happen at any time. To deal with that ultimate fact, human culture is said to develop and offer what may be called a sacred canopy (Berger, 1967). Originally, these belief systems were religious in nature. However, over time people developed various philosophies, social causes, or political ideologies that serve the same purpose: They offer a reason to live beyond a mere desire to survive by providing a clear moral guide or behavioral pathway for living a good, which is to say meaningful, life. Religion, of course, even promises immortality, which, if true, conquers death by transcending it altogether, providing that one faithfully follows its prescribed beliefs and practices whatever they may be.

In this more personal but nonetheless social context, self-esteem is the compass that tells people whether they are on a good moral track in life and rewards them with a clear sense of purpose, meaning, and direction. In addition, straying from the prescribed path also has important affective and behavioral consequences. For example, such negative deviation lowers one's self-esteem, which weakens a sense of purpose or direction and results in making the person more acutely aware of his or her mortality.

This development, in turn, increases his or her experience of angst, which may be manifested in many ways, including anxiety, guilt, and depression, all of which may be associated with low or defensive self-esteem as discussed in chapter 1. Interestingly, the research studies supporting this approach indicate that when people are confronted by stimuli concerning death, those with low self-esteem are more likely to be affected in a negative way. In short, control theories of self-esteem view it as an important emotional signal that helps us govern both individual and social behavior to make it more organized, coherent, and purposeful.

Growth Theories

A third type of theory also accounts for the importance of self-esteem in regulating behavior but differs from the other two in one important fashion. Instead of focusing on maintaining the self or society as the others do, this view emphasizes the role self-esteem plays in human growth and development, especially in regard to the process of self-actualization. Rather than protecting the self or controlling behavior, this approach focuses on how self-esteem is connected to happiness and well-being through the process of self-expansion.

The most well-known version of this view is probably Abraham Maslow's theory because his famous hierarchy of growth is presented in most introductory psychology books. For those who are unfamiliar with it, he placed self-esteem as the fourth of five stages in his theory of development, just below self-actualization. In addition to being one of the first to mention both competence and worthiness in relation to self-esteem, Maslow (1954/1970) understood it as a basic human need as early as 1954. Now there is some empirical support for that position. For example, Sheldon, Elliot, Kim, and Kasser (2001) asked people in Western and Eastern cultures to list satisfying experiences. They found that self-esteem, along with such things as competence, autonomy, and relatedness to others, were most strongly associated with a sense of well-being.

Carl Rogers (1961) went one step beyond Maslow by seeing self-esteem as a central factor in most human development, one that is very much related to the ability to actualize possibilities and to grow interpersonally as well as personally. Growth, it is important to note, involves two processes: giving up the security or comfort of the old and familiar and attempting to reach a new, higher, or at least expanded level of experience, perception, and ability. In other words, growth means taking risks—without guarantees. Not only does self-esteem buffer the individual from the stress of taking these risks, but it actually works to push him or her to do so through that what is known as the *growth tendency*. According to humanistic psychology, this biologically based intrinsic human motivation drives people to actualize their possibilities and "be all they can be" in their personal and relational lives. Consequently, Rogers saw self-esteem as an ongoing process that is with us throughout the entire life cycle, not just as a stage through which to pass, which gives self-esteem a direct connection to well-being.

In sum, it should be clear that each major view of self-esteem has something to offer, namely, forming and maintaining a sense of identity, governing personal and social behavior, and growing or actualizing as a person. In each case, however, the basic function of self-esteem is the same: It is involved in regulating behavior, something that seems to be essential for well-being. Therefore, it makes good sense to know more about the process of self-regulation and how self-esteem is involved in it.

SELF-REGULATION AND WELL-BEING

Self-regulation is a scientific way of describing the processes people use to plan and direct or control themselves emotionally in regard to feelings, cognitively in terms of thoughts, and behaviorally through their actions. Self-control is one of the more obvious expressions of self-regulation, but there are others, such as how individuals participate in the mutual regulation of interpersonal relationships where no one person has complete control. Fortunately, modern psychological research is revealing how the brain works in regard to the processes involved in regulating behavior in these ways.

For instance, healthy self-regulation, which is a larger set of processes than self-control alone, is related to a number of desirable characteristics and behavior. For one thing, people who test at higher levels of this quality generally appear to be better adjusted, experience less psychopathology (mental illness), and have more satisfying relationships than those with less ability to regulate their own behavior. Also, self-regulation is an indicator of future performance, such as in predicting success at school, avoiding undesirable behavior, or reaching higher levels of personal adjustment. However, having good self-control does not mean that one is incapable of relaxing and letting go when appropriate. Rather, like so many other things in life, it is a matter of balance. Simply stated, people who live well seem to know when to hold on and when to let go better than others.

Some of the most exciting research on self-regulation concerns the importance of these processes for our ability to delay gratification. This phenomenon is something we all know about in one way or another, especially if we are parents of young children. For example, in a series of studies by Walter Mischel and his colleagues during the 1970s, a marshmallow was placed in front of young children in a room by an adult (Mischel, Ebbesen, & Zeiss, 1972). The adult told the children that he or she was going to leave the room for a time and would return later. The children were also informed that if the marshmallow placed before them was still there when the adult came back into the room, they would receive two marshmallows instead of just one.

Of course, upon leaving, the experimenters observed the children and noted which ones ate their treat right away and which of them deferred their gratification long enough to wait until the adult returned. This marshmallow test, as it became called for obvious reasons, found that children who were able to exhibit self-control at this early age were likely to be better able to do so elsewhere in life and in adulthood as well. In fact, the children were tracked as they aged, and it was found that those who were able to regulate themselves had fewer behavioral problems, higher grades in school, and higher rates of college acceptance than their more impulsive counterparts.

Several hundred children were involved in the original studies, and much more recently other scientists were able to reassess over 60 of them as adults using a different version of the test (Casey et al., 2011). They compared two groups: those who exhibited high degrees of self-control and those who showed the lowest levels. This follow-up study confirmed the same general findings concerning the value and consequences of self-regulation.

This study is important for several reasons. First, longitudinal research spanning several decades is difficult and expensive to do, which means that it is fairly rare. However, when an idea or concept is confirmed by such work, it becomes more convincing and acceptable. In other words, self-control matters. Second, modern advances in neural imaging also make it possible to observe the areas of the brain concerned with governing behavior. For instance, such techniques make it possible to monitor glucose (a form of sugar the brain uses for its energy) activity in the brain. Scanning clearly indicates that engaging in higher levels of neural processing requires more glucose than lesser states do because such advanced activity requires more energy.

This work shows that higher-level cognitive functions, such as those associated with self-regulation, involve a substantial increase in glucose consumption. Since energy is usually depleted when used, it has been concluded that we have limited capacities to engage in the neural processes associated with positive self-regulation. In other words, good self-control is a limited ability because maintaining it uses up resources faster than they are replenished. In a word, self-control involves real neurological as well as psychological work. One result of this situation is that even the best of us can run out of gas, so to speak, when it comes to positive self-regulation in stressful situations or when trying to maintain a steady focus over long periods of time without rest. Those who have limited capacities or supplies in the first place, of course, are at higher risk of encountering this problem than others.

From this and other work, it is possible to conclude at least three things about self-regulation or control: It is important for well-being, some people are better at it than others, and even those who are good at self-regulation are still vulnerable to lapses. Sometimes I think it is possible to discern when that happens, such as when one becomes physically fatigued while driving and attention suddenly diminishes or when one becomes emotionally drained and then stresses out in one way or another. This research also has important implications for everyday life. For instance, the fact that we all have a limited supply of self-control regardless of our natural abilities means that learning how to manage it more effectively makes good sense for everyone, not just those who have problems in this area.

Self-Regulation and Goal Setting

Some factors that affect self-regulation are easy to see and are well within one's reach, such as good lifestyle habits including healthy diets, regular exercise, adequate rest, and so on. Now modern psychology adds to this knowledge by presenting us with some possibilities concerning self-regulation that are important for increasing well-being as well as authentic self-esteem. One of the most exciting advances concerns key motivational differences between what are called *approach goals* and *avoidance goals*.

Approach goals involve identifying what one desires, looks forward to, and wishes to strive toward because it is in some way attractive. The process of setting and reaching such goals is well understood. Typically, it involves steadily reducing the distance between where one happens to be in relation to the goal at any given time and then taking one more reasonable step in the appropriate direction whenever possible.

Reaching a goal this way has been repeatedly shown to offer several advantages (Harkin et al., 2016), such as only requiring us to focus on the next rung of the ladder, not the entire climb. In other words, setting approach goals allows one to focus his or her neurological, emotional, and behavioral energies on just getting the next step done. Working toward a goal in this fashion is also beneficial because it allows people to see what works and what does not, which is useful in making helpful course corrections. In addition, experiencing even small degrees of progress is beneficial because they provide positive reinforcement, which creates more motivation to keep moving in the same direction until the goal is reached. This process is the scientific truth behind such common-sense sayings as "A journey of a thousand miles begins with a single step" and "Inch by inch, it's a cinch."

Avoidance goals are the opposite. Where approach goals center on taking the next step to reach a goal, avoidance goals split one's attention in two directions. On one hand, the individual still wants to reach the positive goal or outcome. On the other, he or she is also concerned with making sure negative possibilities, such as negative thoughts, self-defeating behaviors, or unexpected distractions, do not occur. Splitting attention and motivation in this way usually detracts from performance because, sooner or later, the individual runs out of the self-regulatory resources necessary for success, such as glucose (more technically glutamate), the ability to concentrate, or patience.

Setting up negative goals may start out with good intentions because reducing unwanted thoughts and responses seems to make good sense. However, such a bifurcation of effort is more likely to reduce the possibility of taking the next step and more likely to increase the likelihood of failure. For instance, when we tell someone, "Don't be so negative," that person must spend self-regulatory resources on the task of monitoring his or her own thoughts and behavior, as well as trying to take the next step toward a positive goal.

M's decision to set avoidance goals instead of approach goals as a child, such as avoiding failure rather than striving for success, is one important reason that the encouragement her parents offered did not work. The irony is that M's decision to concentrate on protecting herself by employing self-handicapping strategies used up mental and emotional energies that could have been better spent on trying harder to succeed. The same scenario is likely to have occurred with her desire to avoid rejection more than to explore possibilities in relationships. In either case, setting negative goals only works for a short time at best and often at the cost of important opportunities for growth, expansion, and well-being.

Traveling to a given location is easier when we have a set destination in mind because approach-oriented goals like this one allow us to better anticipate challenges we are likely to face and to then develop realistic strategies to effectively deal with them. Keeping our mental eyes on the prize, so to speak, requires much less energy than does trying to get there while simultaneously scanning both one's internal and external environment all the time for negative thoughts and emerging threats. In addition, although problem-solving does require mental and physical energies, at least this approach will result in some of the small successes that stand as progress toward the goal, not to mention feeling better along the way.

In fact, the same body of research on self-regulation and goal setting cited earlier shows that people who pursue positive or approach goals also experience lower degrees of stress, less anxiety, and fewer physical complaints than those who build their lives around avoidance goals. All things considered, then, it is better for people to develop a positive, focused plan designed around approaching a desirable goal than trying to avoid things that may happen or may not at any given time. Since this general rule of mental and neurological processing applies to many areas of life, it may be understood as a basic cognitive principle of psychology to keep in mind for effectively managing self-esteem and increasing well-being, both of which will be explored in the second half of the book.

Self-Regulation and the Paradox of Self-Esteem

Self-esteem has been the subject of more than 30,000 books, chapters, and articles (Mruk, 2013a) since it was first introduced to psychology. Much of this work concerns the role of self-esteem in the process of self-regulation, so it is important to recognize self-esteem as a key psychological variable related to well-being, or the lack of it. In addition, there is general agreement among those who research self-esteem that it performs two functions that are crucial for self-regulation. They were first encountered while discussing the basic theories of self-esteem. Examining them more closely can help us to better understand self-esteem, problems with it, and how to increase this valuable personal and interpersonal resource.

By now it should be clear that one function of self-esteem is to help maintain a steady sense of self by protecting one's identity as a competent and worthy individual to whatever extent possible. This aspect of self-esteem is called its *self-protective function* and was first discussed in chapter 1 when I pointed out that even critics of work on self-esteem admit its importance for managing stress. The function, or rather the lack of it, was also seen in the connections between low or defensive self-esteem and various problems of living, ranging from common unhappiness through negative affective conditions involving anxiety to a number of actual mental health disorders. Finally, the maintenance and control theories of self-esteem were seen to center on the importance of establishing and maintaining the stability of the self and identity at the personal or social levels.

As one might suspect from the theories of self-esteem, however, it also helps to effectively regulate personal behavior in positive ways. Just as a lack of self-esteem increases vulnerability to stress, problems of living, and interpersonal problems, for example, its presence has the opposite effect of increasing competence, effectively facing challenges, and maintaining healthy relationships. These more proactive or enhancing personal and interpersonal dimensions of self-esteem are indications of its other major aspect, which is referred to as the *self-expansion function* of self-esteem. As the descriptor implies, this function is more active than reactive (like the self-protective function is) because its purpose is to help people take the risks that are necessary to actualize healthy personal and interpersonal possibilities.

Work in humanistic, developmental, and positive psychology has shown that some degree of risk taking is absolutely essential to develop the skills that are necessary to effectively deal with the challenges of living and thereby grow. Whether the issue is as small as raising one's hand to answer a question in class, as basic as trying one's best in a contest, or as large as quitting a comfortable job to start a new chapter in life, self-esteem helps people realistically assess, trust, and use their abilities to take risks when reasonably appropriate opportunities for growth arise. Similarly, being happy often involves developing a satisfying relationship in which one feels accepted and valued or worthy. Yet to initiate and build relationships, we must risk rejection, which means being vulnerable while at the same time trying to do something that is new or challenging.

The careful reader might notice an interesting contradiction here. On one hand, the protective function of self-esteem motivates an individual to avoid risk and rejection or to at least minimize these possibilities in life. On the other, the self-expansion function pushes people to take risks and thereby become more vulnerable for a time because that is the pathway toward personal or interpersonal growth. When examined more closely, however, what seems like a contradiction is actually an expression of the most dynamic part of self-esteem and how it works.

The desire for stability and the simultaneous need to grow is what allows self-esteem (and identity for that matter) to be reasonably stable and yet open to change. Some people refer to the relationship between these two functions as the paradox of self-esteem because both seemingly contradictory functions actually operate in a dynamic relationship with each other (Bednar, Wells, & Peterson,

1989; Mruk, 2013a). Without this type of active reciprocity, there would be no need to think about gaining or losing self-esteem. Consequently, the inner workings of self-esteem are not just a paradox. Rather, they constitute a paradox that is existentially vital.

Self-Esteem and Motivation

In addition to its two basic functions, some impressive research indicates that self-esteem is also tied to basic self-motivations that all human beings have in common. For instance, Constantine Sedikides (Sedikides, Gaertner, & Cai, 2015; Hepper, Sedikides, & Cai, 2013) found cross-cultural evidence of four basic processes the self employs to sustain its existence. These motivational universals are defensiveness, self-affirming reflections, positivity embracement, and favorable (self) construals.

Defensiveness concerns the ways in which people deal with negative events, including negative feedback from others, that could disrupt a sense of self or well-being. These mechanisms are similar to the classical Freudian defenses that protect people from psychological pain, such as blaming others (displacement and rationalization), but they also include newer ones such as the self-handicapping strategy M readily employs. All of these largely unconscious practices or mental habits help self-esteem shield us from potentially destabilizing stressors.

Self-affirming reflections are another technique individuals use to prevent the destabilization of the self and to maintain a sense of identity. They involve embracing ideological beliefs about the self and others that help manage stress by reducing pain, such as a sense of disappointment or loss. The truisms found in religion, philosophy, or folk wisdom, such as "It happened for a reason" or "Things always work out in the end," might be examples of such helpful affirmations.

A third type of basic self-motivation is something called *positivity embracement* and concerns how people go about getting positive feedback about themselves. There are many ways people may embrace the positive. For example, taking credit when possible (often called the *self-serving bias* in social psychology), associating with others who like or treat one well, and presenting one's best qualities to the world are common ways of maintaining a positive sense of self and self-esteem in this way.

Finally, people may use favorable construals about themselves as individuals to maintain a positive sense of self. As might be expected, there are many ways to construe or construct a positive sense of self as well. For example, we see them in such things as the ceiling effect (which describes how people tend to rate themselves more highly on a desirable attribute than they actually merit) and the tendency most people have to believe that they are above average as a student or worker when compared to others. Being an optimist and believing that the future will be better might be examples of what some psychologists call *positive illusions*, some of which make life more bearable in this way as well.

The careful reader will notice how nicely these basic motivating forces fit with the four types of self-esteem. For example, those with high self-esteem have been found to use self-affirming reflections ("It was meant to be"), positivity embracement ("I can do things"), and favorable construals ("I'm above average") more than do others. As one might expect, people with low self-esteem tend to employ defensive mechanisms (denial and blame) most often because they strengthen one's shield during times of stress or disappointment. Interestingly, however, people with defensive self-esteem, such as narcissists, seem to favor positivity enhancement ("I could do that if I really wanted"), favorable construal ("I'm special"), and defensive (denial and blame) ways of maintaining the self, but not self-affirming responses. The latter characteristic may reflect the difference between feeling one has earned positive feelings about oneself and simply feeling entitled to them.

Further, it is important to note how well these patterns, findings, and related behaviors reflect the basic functions of self-esteem. For example, defensiveness and self-affirming thoughts are ways of protecting the self from stress because they ward off the psychological impact of external assaults to the self by retreating inward to find comfort in things that seem true in ways that do not disturb one's sense of stability. By contrast, seeing oneself in a positive light (favorable construals) and understanding the world as a source of positive experience of one type or another (positivity embracement) open up possibilities in terms of personal and interpersonal well-being in ways that are consistent with the enhancement function of self-esteem.

The practical implications of understanding these additional psychodynamics of self-esteem are also worth appreciating, even if only momentarily. In addition to understanding the functional nature of self-esteem more completely, it might even be worth taking the time to examine which of these four mechanisms one tends to use most as an individual. In M's case, for example, it is clear that she uses several mechanisms, as most people do. However, she does tend to favor defensiveness more than the others as indicated by relying on self-handicapping strategies when faced with a risk and by blaming others when possible. Once such a pattern is identified, it also becomes easier to encourage someone to try using some of the positive strategies more often.

SELF-ESTEEM, POSITIVE EMOTIONS, AND WELL-BEING

Just as low, fragile, or unstable self-esteem can have negative personal and interpersonal consequences, positive and healthy or authentic self-esteem plays a significant role in mental health and happiness or well-being. In general, researchers who study these desirable conditions focus their efforts on two forms of well-being, both of which are related to the phenomenon of flourishing interpersonally and personally. The first type is called *subjective well-being* and usually involves some form of pleasure or enjoyment, which is why it is also known as a hedonic form of happiness. This dimension of well-being includes focusing on things that feel pleasant, such as having a good time, enjoying the company of others, and many forms of activity that are experienced as being fun. Subjective well-being, as one might guess, is a reflection of overall happiness. Most important for our purposes is that people who have authentic self-esteem seem to experience greater levels of subjective well-being and do so more often than others interpersonally as well as personally (Diener & Diener, 1995).

The other type of well-being is more difficult to describe because it involves deeper forms of satisfaction with life that may or may not involve pleasant experiences. Philosophers and psychologists sometimes refer to this type of well-being as the *good life*, one that involves meaning, virtue, and growth. This type of well-being is often based on basic human values that provide a deeper sense of purpose and usually requires hard work, if not genuine sacrifice, to achieve. Positive psychologists often call this type of happiness *eudaimonic*.

Authentic self-esteem plays a major role in both dimensions of well-being, but particularly the latter, because the self-expansion function of self-esteem fosters the ability to be open to new possibilities. In contrast, unhealthy self-esteem—that is, low or defensive self-esteem—narrows one's focus in a way that closes off many possibilities. For example, earlier in her life as a young adult, M was offered the opportunity to receive a full scholarship at a major university. Such a possibility could have been a real boon because she and her parents were of modest means.

However, M turned down the scholarship because she did not feel she could deal with the challenge of maintaining the required grade point due to a lack of faith in her ability, even though the award only required having a 2.0 average. She also "knew" that she was not deserving or worthy of such an award in the first place, which meant that trying to do her best did not warrant the effort it might cost. Like many of us, it became apparent to M later in life that one more measure of competence or worthiness, even a small one, could have given her the courage to take the risks involved. Instead, she was saddled with the regret of not even trying. Such is often the cost of low self-esteem.

Negative Emotions

Charles Darwin was one of the first to note the importance of emotions in regulating animal behavior. Since then scientists, including neuroscientists and psychologists, have continued to study emotions. Most of this considerable body of work concerns negative ones, such as fear, anger, or anxiety, and for very good reasons. For one thing, some of these emotions, particularly those that are associated with the fight-or-flight (sympathetic nervous system) mechanism, are very important for survival, which means that they have high evolutionary value. For example, fear or anger makes an organism focus attention on immediate threats, concentrate its self-regulatory processes on evaluating what possible courses of action may be most protective at that moment, and then prepare to execute the decision to the best of its ability in the hope of survival.

For another thing, negative emotions are often so dramatic and powerful that studying them is relatively easy compared to researching other affective states.

Their physiology or how they work in the body can be readily tested and measured using fairly standard techniques, such as heart rate monitors, respiratory gauges, and so forth. Finally and perhaps even more important, negative emotions, such as guilt or anger, are involved in many forms of human suffering, including mental disorders and aggression. This aspect of negative affect means that studying problematic emotions has a certain priority over other affective states.

Consequently, today we know many things about negative emotions. For example, it is clear that some negative feelings, such as fear, are arousing and thereby mobilize people in a way that increases alertness and the readiness to respond. Negative emotions also help narrow attention to be better able to spot threats in the environment. The adaptive value of these characteristics of negative emotions is that they help people scan their immediate surroundings and prepare strategies for dealing with threats if necessary. Other negative emotions, such as depression or despair, are more problematic because they narrow attention in unhealthy, constrictive ways, such as focusing on problems rather than solutions or on negative events instead of positive ones, which may create greater vulnerability to a host of psychological, physical, relational, and perhaps even spiritual problems.

Positive Emotions

Fortunately, new work in the field focuses on positive emotions too. For example, Barbara Fredrickson's (2002) broaden-and-build theory of emotions shows how positive emotions have substantial evolutionary and practical value. Instead of narrowing attention to focus on what is urgent, Fredrickson found that positive emotions allow consciousness to expand and thereby consider more possibilities. Instead of focusing on a small set of immediate concerns, the open or relaxed states associated with many positive emotions increase one's ability to take in more of the environment.

For instance, the positive form of excitement that comes with emotions of curiosity or those associated with creativity expand our awareness to include, or at least be more open to, imagined possibilities or potential discoveries: Hence, the term *broaden* in broaden-and-build theory. Positive emotions affect the body differently, too. Although some may be obvious, such as the excitement that accompanies joy, the physical effects of positive emotions are often subtle, such as in the quiet pleasure that comes with helping another, talking with a loved one, experiencing gratitude, appreciating beauty, or engaging in meditation.

As much a part of life as they are, however, positive emotions are usually not urgent, and they are seldom problematic. Further, because positive emotions are often subtle, they are far more difficult to study in the laboratory. Consequently, only recently have social scientists begun to focus on positive emotions with any degree of real intensity. Now it is becoming clear that these feeling states are just as important as negative ones because, in addition to adding a more pleasant dimension to an individual's life, positive emotions also seem to have important evolutionary value.

In the most basic sense, we all know the reinforcing power of positive emotions. The pleasure associated with satisfying needs for hunger, sexual activity, and even less physiologically basic things, such as the so-called thrill of victory, all act as positive forms of reinforcement that help individuals stay alive and procreate, thereby ensuring the survival of the species. In other words, positive emotions have evolutional value just as negatives ones do.

Modern neurological and brain-imaging techniques even reveal that much of the reinforcing power of pleasure is located in a particular region of the brain called the nucleus accumbens, which is also known as the pleasure center or the reward center for obvious reasons. Scanning technologies have improved to the point where it is now possible to see that other positive but more subtle emotions, such as curiosity and care, are also rewarding enough to light up parts of the brain in this way. Further, like all emotions, positive emotions also have motivational power. For example, curiosity helps one expand awareness and delay gratification long enough to study a topic until it is mastered or to even endure the sometimes-life-threatening risks associated with exploring new territories. In short, this and other positive emotions help the species, as well as individuals, to evolve or expand.

To date, Fredrickson (2013) identified 10 positive emotions through her laboratory work. Like other emotions, each of them affects thinking and motivates the individual experiencing them to move toward some sort of beneficial goal. In the case of positive emotions, these features are described as a broadening of thinking, creating a positive (approach-oriented) action tendency, and increasing motivation to work in ways that are consistent with what is known about approach goals, not those that involve avoidance as negative emotions might. It is possible to illustrate the similarities and differences between positive and negative using these essential affective characteristics as shown in Table 2.1. Note that I selected a few that were relevant to self-esteem.

Fortunately, Fredrickson did far more than just theorize about the value of positive emotions. She also developed rigorous methods of researching them. For instance, in one experiment she and her colleagues exposed participants in a treatment group to positive visual stimuli of one type or another and then presented them with an activity that required creative responses. According to the broaden portion of the theory, the experimental subjects who received the treatment should generate more possibilities than those in a control group who did not. She did, indeed, find such a connection: The relaxation of attention associated with a positive emotional state seems to facilitate the broadening of cognitive abilities that resulted in the action tendency of seeing more possibilities.

Another experiment involved establishing physiological base lines for subjects by measuring such things as heart rate, respiration, skin conductivity, and the like for two groups of volunteers. After measuring their normal rates, both groups were exposed to negative emotionally stimulating scenarios, such as, perhaps,

Table 2.1. Similarities and Differences between Negative
and Positive Emotions

Negative Emotions	Positive Emotions

Examples of Emotions:
  Fear, Anxiety, Anger
	Examples of Emotions:
	  Hope, Pride, Love

Effect on Attention:
  Narrowing, Sharpening, Focusing
	Effect on Attention:
	  Broadening, Appreciating, Empathizing

Resulting Action Tendencies:
  Arousal, Preparation, Decision-Making
	Resulting Action Tendencies:
	  Openness, Confidence, Acceptance

images depicting violence. After viewing the material, the experimental group was then presented with positive emotional stimuli to experience for a time, while the other or control group encountered emotionally neutral stimuli.

The general result of this experiment and variations on it is that those who were exposed to positive emotional stimuli after encountering negative emotional stimulation returned to their normal base lines of functioning much more quickly than the others. Apparently, positive emotions not only have a broadening affective effect on perception and consciousness, but they also reduce the impact of negative events. Fredrickson and her colleagues called this characteristic of positive emotions the *undoing* effect (Fredrickson, 2002; Fredrickson, Mancuso, Branigan, & Tugade, 2000).

This line of work took Fredrickson to another exciting conclusion. It has long been known that negative emotions, such as stress, can have a damaging cumulative effect over time, one that often results in problematic states affecting health and relationships or well-being in general. Depression is a good example of such a negative emotional trajectory. Once one becomes down or "blue," for instance, it becomes increasingly easy to narrow attention in a way that focuses on negative perceptions, concentrate more on troubling feelings, and then experience a decrease in positive desire or motivation. At some level, brain chemistry is affected in ways that lead to, or are at least consistent with, the chemical imbalances often associated with depression. In other words, we know that negative emotions can create downward self-fulfilling cycles of cognition, experience, and behavior.

Fredrickson reasoned that if both positive and negative emotions involve a related group of cognitive, motivational, and behavioral components that are linked together to produce an overall effect, then positive emotions should also be capable of creating cycles, too. Indeed, she found just that. Thus, the second part of her theory is as important as the first: Positive emotions do not just broaden awareness. They do even more than undo negative experiences. Positive emotions can help us build or expand awareness, see possibilities, and engage in behavior that leads to more of them. In short, she and her colleagues made it clear that positive emotions have the potential to create upward self-fulfilling emotional cycles that increase well-being.

APPLICATIONS

Finally, this work on emotion is advanced enough to suggest some practical guidelines based on the relationship between positive emotions and well-being, some of which are relevant to self-esteem. For instance, Fredrickson and her colleagues concluded that negative emotions are generally stronger than positive ones because it takes several positive experiences to offset the distressing impact of one negative experience, all things considered equal (Fredrickson, 2002). In other words, although it is difficult to make exact comparisons between such things as the intensity, duration, and meaning of an experience, we now have general guidelines concerning how to go about being happier: Strive to have more positive than negative experiences in any given day. Similarly, if one has a very bad experience, then it would make sense to work on having some good ones too. In chapter 6, we shall see that the same dynamic processes accompany emotions and self-esteem in relationships.

Apparently, emotions have the potential to direct us toward similar experiences under certain conditions. In M's case, for instance, self-handicapping began with feeling inadequate about her competence, focusing awareness on the possibility of losing, and then acting in self-defeating ways by holding back her efforts. After enough repetitions, it would not be surprising to find that low and defensive self-esteem can create negative cycles that make it difficult for people to change. Indeed, some people, including M, become so proficient at these ways of perceiving and experiencing the world that few would describe them as being happy. Even worse, it is likely that most people know someone who engages in this type of behavior long enough to engender a genuinely negative or downward self-fulfilling cycle of one type or another. In other words, it is no accident that people with low or defensive self-esteem often find themselves dealing with certain types of problems, such as depression, failure, or poor relationships, again and again.

Just as negative emotions and the self-protective function of low or defensive self-esteem are seen as functioning like a self-fulfilling prophecy that heads in an increasingly gloomy direction, the self-expansion or growth function of self-esteem should work in the opposite direction, similar to the way positive emotions operate. If so, the result would be more of a virtuous cycle or upward self-fulfilling prophecy concerning self-esteem. In other words, one important consequence of authentic self-esteem is that it orients people toward approach goals, which are more compatible with healthy self-regulatory processes.

Actualizing such goals, in turn, should trigger the reward system, thereby creating more positive experiences than avoidance goals would. Increasing the positive emotions associated with being competent and feeling worthy could thereby help facilitate positive upward cycles of self-esteem. If so, then the overall effect should be an increase in mental health and well-being. In fact, this possibility is at the heart of chapters 4 and 5 in which some of the principles of psychology are used to show how it is possible to systematically break a negative cycle of self-esteem and to foster the development of positive experiences instead.

The thought activity presented in Box 2.1a should be helpful in understanding the value of positive emotions in relation to self-esteem. The activity is most easily used with recently experienced positive emotions because these feelings are still active or close to it. For example, it is possible to use the form with M's experience of hope that occurred at various points in treatment to illustrate the activity as presented. Again, a blank form follows the illustration for personal use in Box 2.1b.

Most people tend to focus on large or major positive emotions when doing the exercise, and that is fine. However, there may be more value in learning to appreciate less major or even minor positive emotions because they are much

---

Box 2.1a

THOUGHT ACTIVITY: APPRECIATING THE VALUE OF POSITIVE EMOTIONS

1. Describe the situation in which the positive emotion emerged.
   Admittedly, at first, I thought that working on my self-esteem and well-being would not make much difference. After all, I have been me for a long time, and even though I'm not particularly happy, I've gotten by in life. However, after understanding the difference between authentic self-esteem and just feeling good about oneself, I feel more hopeful.

2. Describe the types of things you experienced, including thoughts as well as feelings during the time the positive emotion occurred.
   It has been a while since I felt hopeful. I guess I have just gotten used to being sort of unhappy or settling for things. But hope feels different. It feels good to see that things don't have to be the same, that there are other possibilities. Hope may not be much, but it does make the future seem a bit brighter and sure beats looking at the negative all the time.

3. Describe the value of seeing, feeling, and acting in the ways that occurred while or after experiencing the positive emotion and how they could help increase well-being in the future.
   Hope is helpful because when I feel this way, I see more possibilities. I know that hope is not the same thing as reality, but seeing more possibilities makes me want to try something new for a change. Hope is not a guarantee, but who knows what might happen. I do know that if I don't try things out, nothing is likely to change. Now, I feel a bit more energized or motivated.

4. Repeat as desired until the ability to identify and appreciate ordinary positive things in life increases enough to affect one's sense of well-being or to at least offset some negative emotions.
   Energized! That is a nice feeling for a change. I guess I need to reflect on feeling excited about possibilities as well. Maybe I should do this activity on a regular basis.

Box 2.1b

THOUGHT ACTIVITY: APPRECIATING THE VALUE OF POSITIVE EMOTIONS

1. Describe the situation in which the positive emotion emerged.

   _____

   _____

   _____

   _____

2. Describe the types of things you experienced, including thoughts as well as feelings during the time the positive emotion occurred.

   _____

   _____

   _____

   _____

3. Describe the value of seeing, feeling, and acting in the ways that occurred while or after feeling the positive emotion and how they could help increase well-being in the future.

   _____

   _____

   _____

   _____

4. Repeat as desired until the ability to identify and appreciate ordinary positive things in life increases enough to affect one's sense of well-being or to at least offset some negative emotions.

   _____

   _____

   _____

   _____

more frequent. For example, an individual who receives an award for an exceptional achievement is likely to experience a very positive sense of self at that time.
But the fact is that such positive moments are also likely to be rare because such
accomplishments are few and far between. Instead of waiting for the next major
self-esteem event to occur, it makes more practical sense to focus on cultivating
smaller or less significant positive moments, such as dealing with a problem well
or being valued by others for making a worthwhile contribution at work or home,
because they are much more likely to occur. In other words, becoming good at
spotting smaller positive events, feelings, and behavior is a more reliable method
of broadening perceptions of ourselves and the world in positive ways. Once
again, practice is important, and it is possible to make this activity a daily event as
well as a part of a self-esteem journal if one is so inclined.

3

Developing Authentic Self-Esteem

If authentic self-esteem helps us effectively deal with stress as well as act as a positive motivational force for living a better life, then there is value in helping people increase their supply of this vital psychological resource. I often use an analogy to help my students and clients understand the existential and psychological importance of authentic self-esteem. It is that self-esteem may be likened to going on a long journey through a desert while carrying a bucket of water. In this case, the desert represents the trials and tribulations of life, and the water stands for the self-esteem that will sustain us through difficult periods until we can reach the next oasis.

To continue the analogy, authentic self-esteem is most desirable because it is potable, dependable, and sustaining. Low or defensive self-esteem are poorer vital supplies because they carry risk, such as scarcity or contamination. Because genuine self-esteem is a precious resource on a journey as long as the life cycle, it behooves the traveler to remember that managing self-esteem well is important. After all, a stumble can cause a spill that slows a journey down, and too many mishaps can lead to a nasty end of one type or another. In addition to caring for the bucket as a container, it is also important to refresh it each time we encounter a potential source of self-esteem. To do that, however, it is necessary to know where authentic self-esteem comes from, which is the focus of this chapter.

SOURCES OF AUTHENTIC SELF-ESTEEM

Acceptance

One could argue that acceptance is the most basic source of self-esteem because it comes first. After all, no one can live very long as an infant without some form of acceptance by others, even if it is only to take care of basic bodily needs. However, the quality of acceptance is important as well. In what is known as the failure to thrive syndrome, for example, it was found that infants who receive sufficient physical attention but who do not receive adequate social interaction (care) often fail to gain weight and then die. This syndrome was noted long ago in extremely crowded orphanages where the staff was simply stretched too thin to hold, cuddle, and interact with babies who then often met this sad end.

A concrete example of how interpersonal relationships are important for the development of self-esteem concerns the ways in which infants develop attachments to their caregivers, especially those who do the mothering. The research on forming these interpersonal bonds concerns how secure (accepted) the infant feels in relation to the mother. The level and type of attachment an infant has is indicated by how much distress is displayed when its mother leaves the room and how quickly relief comes when she returns. The quality of this relationship matters greatly because it influences later personal and interpersonal development. For example, researchers in this area report that those who develop secure attachments during this period fare better in terms of developing higher levels of such important things as independence, secure adult relationships, and, of course, self-esteem (Park, Crocker, & Vohs, 2006).

By contrast, individuals who develop a preoccupied/anxious attachment style are found to be sensitive to rejection and to be more dependent in relationships, while those with a fearful attachment style gravitate toward interpersonal sources of self-esteem, such as needing to be seen as attractive by others. Finally, people with a dismissive attachment style may struggle with interdependence and the ability to make or sustain commitments. Apparently human beings need something more than food and shelter: We need to be connected to others to survive. Being valued enough to warrant interaction and security from others are the most basic forms of human acceptance.

Humanistic psychologists point out that being accepted by others is important for psychological development, especially actualizing one's potentials and relationships. Carl Rogers (1961), for instance, described this form of acceptance as "unconditional positive regard." This way of recognizing the worth of an individual involves accepting the unique combination of characteristics, interests, and potentials that make each person special. The feeling or experience of worth that comes from being accepted by parents and other caregivers is important for self-esteem for two reasons. First, being valued in this way is helpful for development in that it is the very foundation of the worthiness factor in authentic self-esteem.

Second, being accepted as a person of inherent worth or value also sets the foundation for self-acceptance, which humanistic psychologists point out is necessary for the process of self-actualization, for healthy relationships, and for well-being. Imagine how difficult it would be to feel worthy as a person, to accept oneself as a unique individual, or to pursue one's dreams, for instance, if caregivers reject a child, if one doubts his or her basic worth, or if a person tries to follow someone else's dream even if it is a good one.

However, it is important to realize that Roger's (1961) notion is not to be mistaken for accepting anything a child or person does. In fact, the research on parenting and self-esteem indicates that such parental warmth must be accompanied by setting and consistently maintaining high standards for the child to follow as well. It is this combination of factors, not mere acceptance or discipline alone, that fosters the development of authentic self-esteem (Coopersmith, 1967). Again, we see that feeling good and doing good go hand in hand when it comes to self-esteem and well-being.

Caregivers are only the first in a long line of relationships that continue to tell us important things about our worth as a person or the lack of it. This developmental theme continues with relatives, playmates, peers, friends, colleagues, lovers, partners, and, of course, children if one chooses to have them. Indeed, one of the major findings from researchers who study happiness, satisfaction, and well-being is that self-esteem and relationships seem to work together (Diener & Diener, 1995). For instance, people with high self-esteem also report higher degrees of satisfaction in marriage than others, and vice versa.

All that one needs to do to get in touch with acceptance as a source of self-esteem is to reflect on the last time one was lovingly welcomed by family, pleasantly embraced by an old friend, or warmly met by colleagues. Such interpersonal events tell one that he or she is worthy in a way that has a positive impact on self-esteem. Compare those experiences, for example, with the negative impact on self-esteem that often comes with being neglected by family, rejected by friends, or ostracized by colleagues.

In fact, there is an entire literature on what is called *common* or *nonspecific* factors in effective psychotherapy that reveals the power of acceptance in adulthood as well. These factors are the interpersonal characteristics of the relationship between therapist and client that are necessary to make therapy work regardless of the techniques used (Prochaska & Norcross, 1994; Zilcha-Mano, 2017). Warmly and genuinely affirming an individual's worth as a unique human being turns out to be one of the more frequently identified relationship factors that appear in good therapeutic interactions.

Other studies comparing warm (caring) and cold (uncaring) psychiatrists whose duties are largely limited to prescribing medication show that patients who perceive their prescribers as being interested in them as an individual respond better to the same medication than those who do not. Similarly, research shows that whether physicians come across to patients as caring about them matters. Interestingly enough, those who are perceived as warm make the same number of medical errors that colder physicians do, but the warmer physicians are sued less often for their mistakes (Robbennolt, 2008). In short, people never stop responding to genuine acceptance as a source of worth, and they often turn to others to validate it when they cannot see worthiness or value in themselves. Ironically, this source of self-esteem may even come full circle in life if, for instance, one happens to end up depending on the kindness of others to survive in old age.

Virtue

Many social scientists are reluctant to talk about things like virtue and good behavior because they fear being criticized for saying some forms of behavior are right and some are wrong. However, those who study self-esteem found long ago that it is important to appreciate the difference when trying to understand human behavior because another primary source of self-esteem concerns the quality of one's actions in life. Whether the behavior is described as doing that which is just and right, as Milton would have it, or as simply being virtuous, as self-esteem researchers do (Coopersmith, 1967), this source of self-esteem is often more potent than acceptance. Virtue, for example, involves making a worthwhile choice and then acting on it, whereas acceptance is more passive, something akin to receiving a gift from another.

Positive psychologists have pursued the concept of virtue even further and now identify at least six basic types common to the vast majority of major cultures (Peterson & Seligman, 2004). These virtues involve such things as acquiring wisdom in one form or another, being humane toward others, practicing temperance or moderation, appreciating the value of justice, having the capacity to act courageously, and being able to meaningfully transcend the self. Thus, when an individual acts in these more virtuous ways, the person does not simply affirm that which is worthy. He or she also demonstrates his or her merit, value, and character as a human being.

Just as the other side of acceptance is some form of rejection, the importance of virtue for self-esteem is also revealed in its opposite condition. If one fails to act in a way that is virtuous when he or she has a chance to do the right, honorable, decent, or worthy thing, for example, his or her self-esteem suffers and may even drop. Once again, it is easy to get in touch with this source of self-esteem by recalling the last time one either did or failed to do the right thing in a difficult situation. The connection between virtue and self-esteem will come up several times in the book, especially when discussing the relationship between authentic self-esteem and well-being.

Power (Influence)

Another important source of self-esteem comes from having power in life—that is, the ability to influence events in meaningful ways. Like acceptance, the importance of power or influence, depending on which term one prefers to use, also manifests itself early in life, such as when a child attempts to influence events by using a spoon to be in charge of eating or when a toddler radically alters the world by taking those crucial first steps. Developmental psychologists call this form of success *mastery* (White, 1959) because it involves acquiring competencies that are necessary to survive and to grow.

Indeed, Erik Erikson (1983) identified the age of about 6 to 11, the stage of industry versus inferiority, as a time in life during which acquiring competence is crucial to development in most cultures. In ancient times, middle childhood focused on learning basic survival skills, such as hunting, gathering, childrearing, and the like. Today children learn in school how to read, write, do math, become computer literate, and so on, all of which are necessary to master to survive well as an adult in modern society.

However, while learning basic skills is necessary to survive, it is not enough to thrive. Accordingly, continuing to seek, find, master, and exercise power or influence competently in life remains an important source of self-esteem at each stage of the life cycle. For instance, one needs to be competent at dealing with the challenges of living involved in parenting, required at the work place, in dealing with others, and so forth. In addition, people must also develop the competencies involved in learning how to initiate, nurture, and sustain relationships, whether they are at work or in one's personal life. And, of course, it is most important to be able to influence the outcomes of the various and unexpected challenges of living that are sure to come one's way in life.

As an aside, it is often helpful to make a slight clarification concerning the use of the word *competence* in this context because sometimes scientists use a term in more than one way. I always warn audiences when this event happens to avoid unnecessary confusion. In our case, the careful reader may note that competence is being used in two ways.

One is to talk about competence and competencies in relation to power or influence as a source of self-esteem. To be sure, dealing with a particular problem in life does require competence and being successful in this regard does help generate self-esteem, so being competent in regard to mastering a specific task or activity is a genuine source of self-esteem. However, as discussed in chapter 1, competence also refers to one of the two basic components that create and define self-esteem in the first place. This use of the term concerns one's overall ability to deal with the challenges of living and such a global use of the term makes it different from the more specific one just mentioned. In other words, one can be competent at some task or domain of life, which puts one in touch with a particular source of self-esteem, as well as be competent at dealing with life's challenges in general, which pertains to one of the two basic components of self-esteem.

Achievements

The last major source of self-esteem has to do with achievements that are personally significant because they demonstrate competence in an area of life that matters in terms of one's identity as a unique individual. This source of self-esteem is the one James talked about when he began the scientific work in this area. When discussing achievements as a source of self-esteem, people often assume I mean major ones, such as winning a medal, setting a record, closing a lucrative deal, and the like. However, it is important to appreciate the personal part of personal achievements a bit more completely to fully understand how they affect self-esteem.

For instance, one client I knew who had severe developmental disabilities experienced a very high degree of satisfaction in this way the first time he actually dressed himself completely and appropriately—at age 20. For another, it was learning how to brush her teeth by herself, which was expressed by showing off her smile all day. Sometimes hobbies are ways of accessing this source of self-esteem. For example, making something with one's own skill and effort, such as pursuing an intrinsically interesting or valued art or craft, is a type of personal achievement that is good for self-esteem. In this case, the actual level of accomplishment does not matter. Rather, it is being competent at something the individual perceives as worthwhile that counts.

One way to appreciate the opportunities to access the sources of self-esteem available in everyday life is to begin to look for them more actively. Developing this type of awareness is important because of the common tendency to look for dramatic, large, or significant experiences, events, or situations. These more striking *self-esteem moments*, as I like to call them, are valuable and important. After all, dramatic examples illustrate important points well, are easy to recognize, and, most important, can add to authentic self-esteem, all of which are highly desirable. However, major self-esteem moments are also rare, and smaller ones are not. Therefore, if the goal is to understand how self-esteem is actually lived or if the aim is to increase authentic self-esteem, then it makes good sense to appreciate what is more readily available rather than waiting for the occasional epiphany. The thought activity in Box 3.1a uses M's experience to illustrate how to look for the sources of self-esteem in everyday life. It is followed by a blank form in Box 3.1b, which could be another page for the self-esteem journal mentioned in chapter 1 for those who are so inclined.

Connecting the Four Sources with Its Two Factors

The careful reader will note one more important thing about these four sources. A hint is that it concerns our definition of authentic self-esteem. Acceptance and virtue involve some form of worthiness, namely, either being seen as worthy by another or acting in a worthy fashion, respectively. Similarly, success and achievement are clearly connected to competence because they both require mastering skills necessary for successfully facing challenges, both large and small. Thus, we can say that there are only two real sources of self-esteem, namely, those that are based on worth (acceptance and virtue) and those that are connected to competence (success and achievement). Once again, it should be evident that the ability of a two-factor approach to self-esteem is more helpful in integrating what is known about self-esteem than the other definitions can offer.

In addition, both of these primary sources of self-esteem stand in relationship to each other based on the guiding principles of balance mentioned earlier. This dimension of authentic self-esteem is very important to appreciate because all too often people have environments toxic enough to self-esteem that they may not have access to all four sources. For example, some people may be involved with unhealthy, perhaps even destructive, relationships that would make acceptance difficult. Others may not have the resources necessary to influence their environments in a positive way at a particular time in their lives. Fortunately, research consistently indicates that it is not necessary to access all four sources of self-esteem to have it or to increase it (Coopersmith, 1967; O'Brien & Epstein, 1988). According

Box 3.1a

THOUGHT ACTIVITY: IDENTIFYING POTENTIAL SOURCES OF SELF-ESTEEM

1. First, describe an experience, interaction, or situation that involves competence, worthiness, or both. Then reflect on it as a potential source of self-esteem in your life.

   a. Being Valued (Worthiness)
      I stopped by to see a friend in the hospital today to cheer her up as that is what friends do for each other. But in some ways, I may have gotten more out of the visit than she did because when I walked into the room, she seemed so delighted to see me that I felt like the special one. Being valued like that really is a source of self-esteem.

   b. Being Virtuous (Worthiness)
      The boss was picking on Fred again today. Usually, I just kind of look away when that happens. But this time I just couldn't do that because I know the boss was being unfair, so I spoke up for a change. Boy, that wasn't easy because I knew it could come back on me. But sometimes you just have to do the right thing. It made me feel worthy and competent as a person.

   c. Having a Positive Influence on Something (Competence)
      My daughter is at the age when she thinks she knows everything, and I saw her about to make a poor decision. Instead of being the big authority figure and telling her what to do, I let her alone because sooner or later that is what parents have to do. It was really great to hear her say that she knew Mom would not agree with the choice for good reason and then make a better one instead. I guess I have some positive influence on those around me after all.

   d. Personal Achievements (Competence)
      I've been working at this project for several days now. I know it's only a hobby, but when I found the solution to the problem, I felt I really did something of value. Sure, it won't win an award, but it is good to know that I have the ability to be creative and effective when I stick to something.

to the two-factor model, all we need to have authentic self-esteem is to regularly access one source of competence and one source of worthiness at any given time. This information is summarized Table 3.1 for handy reference.

DOMAINS OF WORTHINESS

Another point to make about the sources of authentic self-esteem is that they are strongly tied to everyday life in at least two important ways. First, several

Box 3.1b

THOUGHT ACTIVITY: IDENTIFYING POTENTIAL SOURCES OF SELF-ESTEEM

1. First, describe an experience, interaction, or situation that involves competence, worthiness, or both. Then reflect on it as a potential source of self-esteem in your life.

   a. Being Valued (Worthiness)

   _____

   _____

   _____

   _____

   b. Being Virtuous (Worthiness)

   _____

   _____

   _____

   _____

   c. Having a Positive Influence on Something (Competence)

   _____

   _____

   _____

   _____

   d. Personal Achievements (Competence)

   _____

   _____

   _____

   _____

Source: Modified from Mruk, C. (2013). *Self-Esteem and positive psychology: Research, theory, and practice* (4th ed.). New York, Springer Publishing Company.

Table 3.1. Sources of Authentic Self-Esteem

Competence		Worthiness	
Source:	Power or Influence	Source:	Acceptance or Being Valued
Examples:	Mastery and success; acquiring the skills necessary to influence the direction of one's life or environment.	Examples:	Being valued by others; regarding one's self as worthwhile without being self-centered or narcissistic.
Source:	Personal Achievements	Source:	Acting Virtuously
Examples:	Reaching a personally significant goal or being successful in an area that is tied to one's identity as a person.	Examples:	Honoring something that is worthy, such as knowledge, humanity, justice, temperance, courage, transcendence.
Guiding Principle: Competence must be balanced by worthiness. (One cannot be good at doing bad things and still have authentic self-esteem.)		Guiding Principle: Worthiness must be balanced by competence. (To feel worthy, one must do things that merit such a feeling.)	

social scientists have found that being valued, acting with virtue, expressing influence, and making achievements occur in relatively predictable areas of life called *domains* of living (Harter, 1999; O'Brien & Epstein, 1988). Each such researcher seems to identify slightly different areas, but they can be grouped together without much difficulty. Thus, my approach is to examine this information for regularities to identify the areas that experts consistently recognized as being important for the development of self-esteem. This method results in six general domains of life related to self-esteem that run throughout the lifespan.

Being Connected

Given what we already know about self-esteem and worthiness, it may not be surprising to find that the character, quality, and status of one's relationships with others constitutes an entire domain of life that is important for self-esteem. Both the fields of self-esteem and positive psychology regard being connected to others in healthy ways as essential for well-being. Indeed, those who study well-being even understand the importance of relationships as one of the deep truths of our psychological life (Myers, 2000). Based on the material just covered concerning acceptance, we can certainly say the same: Being valued as a person by others is one area of life that is important for self-esteem.

Feedback concerning acceptance or approval received from others indicates something about whether and how an individual is valued. This information contributes to one's identity and to a person's ability to accept himself or herself, both of which are important for authentic self-esteem and for development in general. In addition, the evolutionary approach to self-esteem maintains that it evolved as a way of helping people be and stay connected to others by regulating behavior in ways that increase chances for survival, including one's own (Leary, 2004).

Fortunately, there are many ways to experience a worthwhile sense of self in this domain of life. They include interactions with family, friends, peers, and so forth. However, since much of development happens in childhood, school is often the focus of such growth and is one reason that good schools will present students with many social opportunities, such as becoming a member of a student council, service club, academic group, athletic team, and so on. As adults, individuals have many opportunities to experience a worthwhile sense of connectedness, such as through parent–teacher associations, neighborhood groups, unions, professional societies, recreational groups, and, of course, volunteer positions of all manners and types. Any of these things and more offer a chance to be accepted or valued by others and to experience oneself as a person of worth.

Physical Attractiveness

As unfair as it may seem, evolutionary and social psychology tell us that such basic characteristics as our physical appearance are important—and not just when we are young (Harter, 1999). It is well known, for instance, that attractiveness plays a role in how we fare in various areas of life. The simple fact of the matter seems to be that one's physical form is what people encounter when they first meet us. Whether it is by the tone of voice, facial structure, body type, physical condition, or even just the way one dresses, people make first and sometimes lasting impressions based on what they encounter through their senses, especially vision. Thus, while some may wish to underplay this dimension of being human in an attempt to be more egalitarian, a basic and somewhat uncomfortable truth of life is that how others react to one's physical appearance matters, even for self-esteem. Hence, it is normal to worry about whether one looks right to peers as children, fits in with a group as an adolescent, makes an impression on dates or job interviews as adults, and is dressed up when expecting visitors in a home for the aged.

No matter who a person happens to be, it feels good when people respond to one's physical embodiment in positive ways because it tells the individual something about his or her social worth. Social psychologists, for example, have long known that, although not without some cost, early maturing boys, physically attractive women, and tall men have something of an advantage in life. Although small, such a benefit may make a difference under certain conditions. Sadly, when compared to average or unattractive people, for instance, social scientists have found that attractive people are often judged to be more honest, more intelligent, more mentally healthy, and so on than less fortunate others. Attractive people even seem to be paid more for similar work than their unattractive counterparts, and attractive people appear to be found guilty in court less often as well. Fortunately, authentic self-esteem moderates this effect because it involves more than this domain of life and because there are other sources of worthiness, such as virtue or moral character. However, it is still interesting to note that of all the domains affecting self-esteem, researchers suggest that this one appears to change the least over the course of the life cycle.

Morality and Virtue

Except perhaps for people with very disturbed levels and types of self-esteem, such as narcissists and psychopaths, most of us learn to value that which is good, desirable, and worthwhile from parents, religions, schools, books, plays, television, and, yes, sometimes even the Internet. Similarly, most people come to develop positive or healthy personal values that are meaningful to them as unique individuals. In addition to acquiring such standards of worth, most people try to honor them as well, even if only in the way the terror management theory suggests. When people do that, their sense of worth tends to go up and when they don't, that is felt too, usually in the form of regret, guilt, or shame.

The connection between virtue and self-esteem often occurs in regard to making decisions, especially those that pertain to personal and social regulation. The range of such decision-making is impressive. For example, it can involve something as small as making a choice about whether to take a second dessert to something as large as standing up for the rights of another when one witnesses them being abused. How one regulates himself or herself when responding to such moral dilemmas can have great meaning for self-esteem, particularly one's sense of worth as a person (or the lack of it, depending on what one decides to do). Because virtue often involves decision-making as well as action, it is trying to do the right thing that matters, sometimes even more than the outcome. Giving one's best effort is an affirmation of worth whether one is successful, though being successful has the additional value of adding competence to the picture. Indeed, because both factors can be involved in facing a challenge of living that requires being virtuous to resolve well, these self-esteem moments are among the most beneficial to developing authentic self-esteem.

DOMAINS OF COMPETENCE

Problem-Solving Abilities

Much of life involves dealing with problems, perhaps most of life for that matter. However, there is much more to this domain than success or failure. For one thing, solving problems involves certain cognitive abilities. Assessing what is needed in a given moment, deciding where to apply one's efforts in a particular situation, and believing in one's ability to succeed, or what psychologists sometimes call *self-efficacy*, are all examples of the mental processing found in solving problems. Of course, having the actual skills to effectively deal with the challenge is not the same thing as merely believing one has the ability to do so, which is why it is important to distinguish between authentic self-esteem and self-efficacy. In other words, while self-efficacy and/or self-confidence are a part of authentic self-esteem, they are not all that is involved in being competent: Actual ability is another and so is motivation.

The ability to solve problems matters for self-esteem because success and failure are related to competence. Thus, whether they involve the self, other people, or some external condition in the world around us, problems that affect one's values, interests, and especially identity are most important for self-esteem. These challenges of living are found in such things as learning how to acquire the basic skills necessary for completing school, earning a living, developing abilities necessary to advance a career, discovering how to communicate well in a relationship, finding out how to be an effective parent, and so on. The particular problems that affect people in this way change with age or circumstance, but it is clear that the theme of problem-solving and its subsequent meaning for self-esteem will always be a part of life.

Autonomy and Control

The ability to have an active voice in one's life also pertains to self-esteem and well-being. Sometimes people use the word *autonomy* to describe this dimension of self-esteem because autonomy involves having a sense of what one would like to do in a given situation, as well as some degree of control or influence to make that happen. For example, it has been found that even monkeys tolerate stress better when they have some control over it. Similarly, other research shows that those who are capable of exerting some influence on events, such as corporate CEOs or physicians, have less stress-related illness than those with little control, such as secretaries or nurses. Of course, the particular areas of life where having influence makes a positive difference may differ with personality, circumstance, or age, but, in general, autonomy is also related to well-being. As mentioned before, for example, autonomy is found to be one of the most satisfying experiences people have across cultures (Sheldon, Elliot, Kim, & Kasser, 2001).

Autonomy is connected to self-esteem in a number of ways, but they usually center around three factors: intrinsic values, self-expansion, and risk-taking. Well-being is connected to one's degree of awareness concerning what is valuable to him or her as a unique individual. These *intrinsic values*, as they are called, motivate the person to actualize possibilities associated with them. The result of following these values creates a sense of direction or purpose in life that, when fulfilled, becomes a source of meaning and satisfaction, which contributes to well-being. However, actualizing possibilities involves risks, such as the possibility of failure or rejection, which can threaten, affect, or even alter identity.

Fortunately, the two regulatory functions of self-esteem can work hand in hand in these risk-taking situations. When an appropriate opportunity arises, for instance, the possibility of expanding the self or growing as a person becomes more attractive, thereby motivating the individual to move in that new direction. Competence is important because it makes this process easier and increases chances of success. However, worthiness is active too, because it buffers us against the experience of failure or rejection, which is an inevitable part of the process of actualizing the good things in life. Most people can probably recall a time when they were on the verge of success and it felt like all that they needed to do was to take one more step to get there. In this situation, authentic self-esteem can make the difference between success and failure. While most of us can probably also easily identify times we were able to snatch defeat from the jaws of victory, to paraphrase an old cliché, the work on positive emotions indicates it is much healthier to focus on the times one did manage to actualize a meaningful possibility by taking a leap of faith in oneself.

Physical Integrity

The last general domain of life that pertains to self-esteem also concerns well-being: one's physical abilities and possibilities. As children, people often cannot wait to grow up because they know that, as their bodies mature, their abilities increase in ways that open up more possibilities in life. This tide turns in adulthood when individuals begin to encounter the limits their bodies present in any number of ways. In fact, all one needs to do to appreciate the importance of this dimension of self-esteem is to recall what happens to one's sense of competence, and sometimes even worth, when suffering from an illness or recovering from an injury.

Indeed, one of the greatest blows to self-esteem and well-being can come from serious or incapacitating physical injuries or limitations. Often people who suffer such conditions must deal with their self-esteem before they can recover or effectively adapt to the change. For the rest of us, simply getting older involves milder doses of the same challenge, confirming the importance of physical functioning for both self-esteem and well-being over time.

Connections between the Domains and Self-Esteem

Again, the careful reader will note several things about these six major domains of life affecting self-esteem, and vice versa. One is the relationship between self-esteem and well-being. Each domain or dimension of life can be lived in ways that either increase well-being by doing them right or decrease it by doing them poorly. For example, one can take good care of relationships to help facilitate genuine acceptance. It is possible to maximize attractiveness in reasonable ways when doing so is appropriate or helpful. Most people know the importance of being virtuous and at least try to do the right thing most of the time. Almost everyone wants to master the problems he or she encounters in life at least to some extent. Autonomy, it will be remembered, was identified as one of the most satisfying experiences and may even stand as a basic human need. Finally, most people appreciate their physical abilities, although there can be some very challenging ways to learn about their value.

Next, it is also clear that all of these domains are connected to at least one of the two basic factors associated with authentic self-esteem. For example, being connected to others, being accepted physically, and honoring virtue are strongly associated with a sense of worth or worthiness. Problem-solving, autonomy, and physical integrity clearly involve some form of competence. Of course, it often occurs that both factors are involved in a specific domain, which is also consistent with defining self-esteem as a relationship between competence and worthiness. For instance, sometimes how one plays the game or goes about pursuing a goal is often just as important as winning or reaching it.

Each of these domains has general as well as specific developmental importance because they are with us throughout the entire lifespan. In addition, none of the domains exists by itself. Since they are all basic dimensions of life, they often interact with each other in various modes of reciprocity. For example, competence may be influenced by physical ability, and worthiness may be responsive to various genetic traits, such as extroversion, which tends to push one toward having a greater number of interactions with others and increases the possibility of developing relationships.

Finally, several studies indicate that self-esteem actually has a relatively predictable trajectory that runs through the life cycle. In fact, this research shows that typically self-esteem is high in childhood; drops somewhat in adolescence, especially for some females (Harter, 1999); and then slowly but steadily rises in early adulthood to about age 60 or so when it levels off, though self-esteem may decline with illness or poverty (Trzesniewski, Robins, Roberts, & Caspi, 2004). Consequently, it may be best to see self-esteem as a lifelong developmental issue that is very much connected to one's overall well-being.

In other words, although the names of the specific tasks and challenges associated with each domain can and do change with age, they never leave. For example, social roles and interactions change from childhood, through adulthood, and in aging, but they still can form the basis for relationships and, therefore, a sense of worth. Problem-solving moves from learning how to control body functions, to playing games, earning a living, raising a family, and, sometimes, back to mastering basic functions again. However, the theme of solving problems and its connection to competence as well as self-esteem never goes away.

Of course, it is also important to recognize that there is a high degree of individuality associated with each of these domains. Although everyone deals with the same basic stages and developmental challenges over time, no two people ever go through the process in an identical fashion. What becomes thematic, interesting, or problematic in a given domain for one person might be background noise, boring, or unpleasant for another. In fact, it probably isn't possible to even list all of the different possibilities in one domain, not to mention those that exist in all six. As James (1890/1983) so definitively pointed out, it is the areas of a given domain that are involved in an individual's sense of identity that matter for self-esteem, not the domain itself.

Similarly, it is very important to point out another cardinal rule of development that applies to self-esteem and that is the idea of *good enough*, which was proposed by Donald Woods Winnicott (1953) long ago. The idea is simple but powerful. Research on what is known as *resilience* shows that, without a doubt, things do not have to be perfect for us to do well in life (Vaillant, 1998). For instance, although the brain needs a certain amount of protein to grow normally, it need not come from a daily diet of lobster and steak. All the brain needs is a proper balance of proteins and amino acids, which can be provided by a number of foods in combination with each other. Likewise, children do not need perfectly loving and caring parents to develop fully as human beings. In other words, just because a person had poor parents does not mean the individual is fated to grow up to be a poor adult or doomed to having a poor life. All people require is *good enough* parenting from an aunt, uncle, grandparent, foster parent, neighbor, or teacher, and they can do quite well developmentally and otherwise in life. The same is true for accessing the sources of self-esteem.

Earlier I said that these six themes run throughout the life cycle because people deal with the challenges they present at each phase of life. Further, almost everyone will develop difficulties that affect self-esteem in one or more domains crucial for identity that turn into problematic self-esteem issues or themes. Finally, it was noted that there is tremendous variation in how each individual deals with these six domains of life, as is the case with any developmental phenomenon. These variables are different and complex enough to generate some confusion, so a brief illustration may help clarify them. One experientially oriented way to do that is to look at the thought activity in Box 3.2a using M's experience and then to try out the blank form in Box 3.2b. Again, this material may simply be read and reflected upon or could become a part of a self-esteem journal, depending on inclination.

It is important to recognize such qualities as potential strengths an individual possesses because they are grounded in reality, which gives them substance and makes them difficult to deny or discount. Knowing about these characteristics is potentially helpful to those interested in increasing authentic self-esteem, so it may be worth taking the time to develop a list of one's own positive qualities in each domain and to reflect on them. On another note, this type of information may also be helpful in fostering the development of healthy self-esteem or for dealing with budding self-esteem problems earlier in life. As might be expected, for example, I train some teachers in this approach as well as therapists who work with children and adolescents. Although this book focuses on self-esteem in adulthood, I see no reason why paying attention to a child in each or all of these domains would not be advantageous. In other words, increasing competence and worthiness can be preventative measures in addition to being a focus of treatment.

Box 3.2a

Thought Activity: Domains of Self-Esteem

A. Worthiness-Based Domains

1. Being Connected: Relationships in your life that seem to bring a sense of acceptance/worth.
   Like most people, I have a few close friends who accept me for who I am in spite of my faults. Some of my family members and colleagues at work see me as worthwhile too.

2. Physical Attractiveness: Things about your appearance or presence that receive compliments.
   I have very smooth skin and a clear complexion that people comment on in positive ways. I look pretty good in certain types of clothing too.

3. Morality and Virtue: Times in life or areas in which you maintain a high degree of integrity.
   Although not perfect, I usually try to do the right thing, especially when it comes to being a good parent. When wrong, I am usually able to admit my mistakes, take responsibility, and fix them.

B. Competence-Based Domains

1. Problem-Solving Abilities: Your particular skills and abilities.
   People at work seem to see me as the "go-to" person when they have a problem fixing anything mechanical. I guess I do have some ability in that area, and it makes me feel creative as well.

2. Autonomy and Control: Areas in life where you have a voice, influence, or make decisions.
   One of the reasons I work well on my own is that it gives me the ability to evaluate things my way and come up with better solutions. Maybe that is why I get special projects at work.

3. Physical Integrity: Positive abilities based on your age, gender, and abilities.
   Well, I may not be in top physical shape, but I watch my diet, exercise regularly, and can certainly do most of the things people my age do, and sometimes even more!

Box 3.2b

THOUGHT ACTIVITY: DOMAINS OF SELF-ESTEEM

A. Worthiness-Based Domains

1. Being Connected: Relationships in your life that seem to bring a sense of acceptance/worth.

   _____

   _____

2. Physical Attractiveness: Things about your appearance or presence that receive compliments.

   _____

   _____

3. Morality and Virtue: Times in life or areas in which you maintain a high degree of integrity.

   _____

   _____

B. Competence-Based Domains

1. Problem-Solving Abilities: Your particular skills and abilities.

   _____

   _____

2. Autonomy and Control: Areas in life where you have a voice, influence, or make decisions.

   _____

   _____

3. Physical Integrity: Positive abilities based on your age, gender, and abilities.

   _____

   _____

THE IMPORTANCE OF SELF-ESTEEM
MOMENTS AND TRAPS

The last point to consider in the development of self-esteem according to the two-factor approach is the most important one for our purposes because many things we know about self-esteem seem to tie into it. This aspect of self-esteem has to do with the way people face the challenges that emerge in the six domains of life that have a direct impact on self-esteem or its development. Situations that call into question one's competence or worthiness have meaning for identity as well as self-esteem because they put people *at stake* in these ways, as William James (1890/1983) said. In other words, how one handles these particular self-esteem moments affects who one is as a person and how he or she lives his or her life. The fact that these self-esteem related domains affect identity makes self-esteem even more important. That is why some researchers consider self-esteem to be a pivotal variable in determining a person's behavior (Rosenberg, 1965).

Although each domain presents opportunities for success or failure and worthiness or rejection, there are three sets of experiences that seem especially important for self-esteem. First, providing it is genuinely worthwhile and not harmful, destructive, or demeaning, demonstrating competence creates a type of self-esteem moment that brings a sense of satisfaction and well-being to an individual. In a word, we earn the sense of competence that comes with these experiences and the corresponding impact they have on self-esteem.

Second, there are other times in life when we feel appreciated, accepted, highly valued, or even loved by another human being. This class of self-esteem moments affects the worthiness component of self-esteem in a positive fashion. It simply feels good to be recognized as a person of worth in these ways, sometimes deeply so. Of course, rejection, loss, or abandonment, and the like also have an impact on worthiness in the opposite fashion, which diminishes one's sense of value as a person, and that is felt as well. All one has to do to get a sense of how either competence or worthiness affects self-esteem is to recall positive or negative experiences one has had in either area, just as we did in a previous thought activity. Again, however, I recommend focusing on the positive ones more than those that are negative because positive tends to beget positive, as it were.

It may be helpful to recall that there is good empirical support for this way of understanding and valuing the two types of self-esteem moments discussed so far. For example, Seymour Epstein (1979) asked a good number of participants to record the experiences that seemed to affect their self-esteem in positive and in negative ways for an extended period. The participants reported that successes and failures, as well as starting and ending relationships, seemed to have the most impact on self-esteem—just what should be expected from a two-factor approach.

The developmental fact of the matter is that, beginning in childhood and not ending until one dies, individuals establish an existential record of positive and negative self-esteem moments. In Western cultures, we call this the running total self-esteem, though other cultures may have different words for it. For example, a graduate student working with me on self-esteem happened to be a Native American. He pointed out that, although his people did not have a word for *self-esteem* as psychologists use the term, they recognize those who live a high degree of competence and worthiness without any difficulty—as well as those who do not.

Crossroads of Self-Esteem

The third major type of self-esteem moment is the most important because it offers the greatest potential for change. This one stems from a situation that challenges a person's competence and worthiness at the same time and on two levels. Although such self-esteem moments are more complex, some of us studied them enough to find that they have the potential to dramatically alter self-esteem in a positive or negative direction, depending on how one resolves the challenges they present (Jackson, 1984; Mruk, 2013a). Continuing with the analogy, it can be said that negative outcomes during such times in life may create holes in the bucket of self-esteem, which results in its loss. However, positive experiences of this type not only increase authentic self-esteem in the moment but also may even repair leaks in the bucket, which bodes well for the future.

Sometimes these challenges are very clear, such as when we are faced with making a choice between what we know is right and wrong in a particular situation. For instance, having the opportunity to cheat to win or to make oneself look good by unfairly taking credit for something another has done at work are fairly straightforward examples to consider. In these cases, showing that one has the right stuff (the reference to Milton is intended) is an important expression of competence when dealing with the challenges of living that simultaneously demonstrates one's worth or integrity as a person. Failing to meet the challenge, or even just giving it less than one's best efforts, indicates something very different about an individual and has a correspondingly negative impact on self-esteem. As I've said before, authentic self-esteem is earned, not given, which means that it can be lost as well as won.

However, sometimes self-esteem challenges trigger problems with competence or worthiness that run deeper in a person's life than the issues associated with the immediate situation. This dimension or level of challenge arises only when two conditions are present. The first is that a person finds himself or herself faced with a choice about whether to do that which is worthy, clearly knows it, and very much wants to do the right thing. The second is that making the worthy choice requires the individual to deal with an additional obstacle, one that is grounded in self-esteem struggles of the past. In other words, this third type of self-esteem moment forces the individual to contend with unresolved issues associated with one or more of the six self-esteem domains. In this case, making the decision that is just and right for the first or surface level of challenge also involves reexperiencing and dealing with a personal fear or weakness on the second or hidden level. That is why I call these self-esteem moments a *crossroad of self-esteem*.

For example, being in a situation with a bully that challenges one's competence and worthiness is one test of a person's self-esteem. However, being in the same situation and having a history of always avoiding or cowering in similar circumstances since childhood is another degree or level of challenge. Standing up for oneself in any self-esteem related domain of life is much more difficult if one has historically repressed one's intrinsic values or typically caves in to the desire to avoid dealing with one's own issues.

These developmentally problematic self-esteem themes inhibit an individual's ability to make a healthy response, which is why they may be described as *trapping* self-esteem. Most people have such problematic self-esteem themes. However, it may be more difficult for those with defensive self-esteem to see their traps because some forms of self-protection often feel oddly good or at least bring a temporary feeling of relief associated with denial. Such self-protective behaviors as intimidating others or humiliating them when they criticize one's work may be examples of such behavior. Psychologists point out that this secondary gain only makes facing oneself more difficult in the long run.

Fortunately, research on self-esteem moments also reveals that each time a challenge of living activates such a problematic self-esteem theme in the here and now, the situation also brings with it a fresh opportunity to do something different (Jackson, 1984; Mruk, 2013a). Freud called this dynamic the *repetition compulsion*, which is a way of saying that once these themes become a part of an individual's psychological life, he or she is doomed to repeat them until the underlying issue is fully confronted. Others might describe this cycle of repeating a lesson until it is mastered as a type of psychological karma because facing the issue is linked to one's ability to move beyond it to higher developmental levels.

In other words, the particular self-esteem moments that arise due to this set of dynamics are a psychological gift: Each time they emerge, people have an opportunity to break psychological chains of the past, heal developmental wounds in the domains of life associated with self-esteem, and free themselves from the bondage of low or defensive self-esteem in the present and for the future. Humanistic psychologists understand transcending the past in this way as a form of *authenticity* because it involves having a higher degree of self-awareness, knowing what is at stake existentially, being willing to accept responsibility for one's actions, and mustering up the courage to do one's best. As will be discussed in the next chapter on changing self-esteem, they are right.

Authentic self-esteem, then, involves courage because sometimes it is necessary to face fear, not just uncertainty, to grow. Indeed, the lack of courage often contributes to the development of problematic self-esteem in the first place. For example, M demonstrated such a problem by opting for the comfort offered by using self-handicapping solutions even though they contributed to failures. She also failed when she lacked courage to face the challenge of standing up for herself in relation to others in certain situations as an adolescent. Most of us can readily

Box 3.3

Ten Common Self-Esteem Themes and Traps

A. Worthiness-Based Traps
1. Having difficulty feeling good enough in relation to others or frequently feeling inferior, inadequate, or ashamed.
2. Depending too much on others to feel good about yourself, including excessively seeking praise, being too concerned with pleasing others, or being afraid to be alone.
3. Having the same types of problems in relationships over and over, including difficulties feeling accepted by another or, conversely, with allowing them to genuinely care for you.
4. Bragging, having to show others that you are better than them, putting others down, or even bullying others.
5. Repeatedly doing things that you know are not good for your body, mind, relationships, or spirit and then feeling bad afterward.

B. Competence-Based Traps
1. Preferring to avoid conflict, even if it means putting up with activities or treatment you don't like or want.
2. Wanting to do something that is important to you, but handicapping your chances by focusing on the negative, not trying your best, or avoiding opportunities.
3. Reacting too defensively to criticism of your work or suggestions concerning your behavior when the feedback is clearly not meant as an attack.
4. Having to prove yourself as always being the best, always being first, or always being right, and getting upset with yourself or others when you are not.
5. Finding yourself dominating, manipulating, or taking advantage of others because it makes you feel better about yourself.

---

identify some similar problematic self-esteem themes in our own lives. For instance, sometimes I encounter in my work as a professor students who, based on their early school experiences, underperform, and sometimes even drop out, because they believe that they are too stupid to pass a course.

To help others understand and identify the various types of self-esteem traps people often face, I created a list of 10 common problematic self-esteem themes that often present such difficulties in Box 3.3. The list is not exhaustive, to be sure, but it does organize the traps into those that primarily involve problems with worth and those that largely stem from difficulties with competence. As might be expected, often there is some degree of overlap as the two factors affecting self-esteem always stand in relationship to each other.

Most people with self-esteem problems could probably fill a book with stories about how they failed here or how rejection occurred there. However, the research on positive emotions examined earlier clearly indicates that there is a much better alternative. As we saw in chapter 2, it is best to focus on the positive because doing so undoes some of the damage from the past, broadens possibilities in the present, and may help prepare the way for an upward cycle in the future. Since this book is concerned with things in life that contribute to self-esteem and well-being, I take this approach in the next two chapters and show how M broke free of her self-esteem traps in meaningful ways.

4

How to Increase Authentic Self-Esteem

First, previous chapters showed the two-factor approach to self-esteem reveals four types, only one of which is authentic. Next, it became clear that self-esteem is paradoxically dynamic in that it works to both protect the self in times of need and yet expand one's sense of identity and well-being whenever possible. Then we examined the sources of self-esteem as well as its development, which included six domains of life and the importance of self-esteem moments within them. This work provides the scaffolding for the aim of the book, which is to help people find reliable ways of increasing authentic self-esteem to enhance well-being.

The regulatory functions of self-esteem make it important for everyday life, especially in regard to dealing with stress. Consequently, some therapies try to increase self-esteem by uncovering deep-seated problems in the hope that resolving unconscious conflicts will create a stronger shield. However, since well-being involves the expansion function of self-esteem more than its protective function, developing a method of change that focuses on the present is more consistent with the two-factor approach. In other words, increasing authentic self-esteem in the here and now helps people develop a better sense of worthiness and a higher degree of competence concerning their ability to deal with the challenges of living as they actually arise.

One way to do that is known as competence and worthiness training (CWT; Mruk, 2013a), which is an approach to increasing authentic self-esteem I developed over the last 30 years. This program is based on the upper right-hand quadrant of the self-esteem matrix presented in chapter 1, the only one that is characterized by a high degree of both self-esteem factors. In addition to being a positive form of therapy (Mruk, 2008), this program has two other features that make it relevant here. First, CWT has been studied by other researchers who found it to be reliable and valid and then reported these findings in published work (Bartoletti, 2008; Hakim-Larson & Mruk, 1997; Hunt, 2010). Second, CWT can be modified to fit a more educational format that may be helpful for increasing well-being and authentic self-esteem for people in general, not just clinical populations. This aspect of the program is important for our purposes because it means that the method can be applied to everyday life.

Returning to the bucket analogy for a moment, it can be said that taking a long journey through an arid region is a major challenge of living. A good traveler tries to add water to the bucket each time he or she comes across a potential source of it. For instance, if one happens to stumble across an oasis, something akin to experiencing a major self-esteem moment, it is important to take advantage of the opportunity and fill the bucket as much as possible. However, an even wiser person will learn how to effectively manage that bucket right from the beginning because this individual knows that oases are rare and that one is sure to experience spills and accidents from time to time on a long enough journey. Thus, like occasional rains in the desert, small self-esteem moments are important too. As I've said before, it is prudent to be mindful of small self-esteem moments because they occur more frequently in life and can add up to have a positive effect on well-being over time. Of course, it is also common sense to avoid as much as possible making choices that risk spilling the precious psychological resource called self-esteem.

BREAKING FREE OF WORTHINESS-BASED SELF-ESTEEM TRAPS

The first method that has proven useful for helping people take small but steady steps toward increasing authentic self-esteem involves learning how to identify habits of mind that unnecessarily lessen one's sense of worth as a person and how to prevent that from happening. For example, one of the most common yet important self-esteem traps is poor mental hygiene concerning one's experience and perception of who one is as a person. Cognitive psychologists and other mental health professionals have various names for such negative and self-fulfilling mental habits, such as engaging in distorted, dysfunctional, or irrational thinking. The college students who saw themselves as less worthy just because they did not get into a favored school are an example of distorting reality in these ways.

This body of work demonstrates that once these negative cognitive patterns become a part of one's self-experience, they create powerful feedback loops that painfully amplify the significance of cognitive errors people often make concerning such things as mistakes, setbacks, weaknesses, and unsatisfying interpersonal moments. As we saw with M, constantly recycling these types of events create negative habits of mind that diminish one's ability to see the world, self, and future in more positive or at least realistic ways. In other words, becoming very good at very poor mental habits can trap self-esteem in ways that decrease well-being. This possibility is the grain of truth in the old adage about seeing a glass as half-empty, though in reality it is also half full.

Some people (Durand & Barlow, 2015) call this perception of the world, self, and future a *negative cognitive triad* or *schema* (schematic, like a blueprint) and we know much about how these habits of mind work. For instance, the plasticity of the brain is such that neural sculpting forms patterns of processing information that govern perception, experience (including self-experience), and problem-solving. Once these processes become set, they begin to automatically filter information, often without awareness, which makes them difficult to stop. As M discovered, if the patterns one uses to make sense about how the world works and what the future will be like become distorted, then life may become much harder than it needs to be—and it is often difficult enough.

Various researchers have identified at least 20 such negative patterns the brain uses to process information incorrectly in this way and some of them concern distorting one's sense of self. Upon examining such lists, I have found that five terms are used most often to describe negative thinking patterns or habits of mind that lower a person's sense of worth, so I focus largely on these self-esteem traps in my research and therapeutic work (Mruk 2013a, p. 263).

1. *Overgeneralizing*: This mental distortion was probably the first one to be discovered and researched in cognitive psychology. The word is very clear: It means to take what has happened, in this case a negative event or situation, and drawing negative conclusions from it about one's worth as a person that extend way beyond what is realistic. Jumping to unfounded conclusions is one way to overgeneralize. So is making doom-and-gloom predictions about the future based on a single negative event or outcome. Unfortunately, the tendency to believe in erroneous conclusions or to worry about unlikely futures cuts off more positive possibilities, thereby limiting one's range of self-experience and behavior. Saying something to oneself such as, "I know I will fail because I always do" would be an overgeneralization.

2. *Filtering*: Many cognitive or mental traps involve distorting reality in ways that make it seem much worse than it is, something that causes more suffering than is necessary. The most common way to make such a distortion is to simply focus attention on the negative aspects of a situation or event by minimizing or even leaving out positive possibilities. Sometimes this trap is called "making mountains out of molehills" or "catastrophizing," both of which turn mistakes, setbacks, or disappointments into disasters in one's mind. Giving a good speech and then telling people one did a terrible job because of a mispronounced word or simple mistake might represent this type of filtering.

3. *Labeling*: Sadly, many people learn to call themselves highly distorted and very negative names that almost always detract from a sense of worth. Labeling oneself as a *loser, wimp, stupid, fat, ugly,* and so on are some of the most painful self-esteem traps because they affect identity itself. As such, they only add unnecessary suffering to situations that are often already painful or disappointing. It is one thing to make a mistake, for example, and another to call, see, or experience oneself as being a stupid person over what is actually only an error. Even worse, with enough practice, such a processing pattern can become self-fulfilling.

After all, stupid people must do stupid things to be truly stupid, and they must do them much more often than others.

4. *Personalizing:* Sometimes an individual may simply be too sensitive. It is not that sensitivity is a bad thing. In fact, it is necessary to be sensitive to events and to others to develop empathy or care. However, people with low or defensive self-esteem tend to lack a healthy buffer or sturdy shield so they often overreact to negative events by taking them far too personally. In some cases, such a person may even react to things that are not necessarily real. For example, the individual may feel that a friend who failed to wave hello back is angry at him or her when all that really occurred was that the other person was preoccupied with an upcoming event, such as an exam. Sadly, personalizing is a very common way of feeling worthless that adds unnecessary pain to one's life.

5. *Emotional Reasoning:* Emotional reasoning is a particularly tricky way of making things seem worse than they are because it involves being trapped in an endless loop. It begins with feeling bad about something but instead of accepting reality and realistically dealing with it, the person gives in to his or her emotional reactions and lets negative feelings dominate the picture. This response is a trap because once one falls into it, getting out is difficult, something akin to an emotional roller coaster where just as one begins to relax, the ride starts all over again. In other words, emotional reasoning is a repetitive cycle of negative thoughts, perceptions, and feelings with little in the way of an off switch. The clearest indication of when an individual is trapped in this way can be seen when the person is just about ready to respond in a mature fashion and then suddenly thinks or says something like, "Yeah, I see it's not that bad, but . . . " or "If only this or that wouldn't have happened, then I wouldn't . . . " This type of irrational thinking pulls people back from the brink of healthy realism into a cognitive cycle of suffering.

Neuropsychologists and others now describe the brain in terms of its plasticity because it can adapt to new situations all the way from learning how to throw a ball to recovering from a stroke. Cognitive psychologists often describe how one of the primary functions of the brain is to identify and recognize patterns. If so, it is reasoned, then it should be possible to alter thinking patterns based on the same general principle, namely, the ability to adapt to new stimuli and reorganize neural and perceptual processes to create new or more effective ones. The therapeutic application of this approach is variously called *cognitive restructuring, reframing, rewiring the brain, training the brain,* and the like. Regardless of the name or who is describing these processes, the aim is to help people break out of old, unrealistic, or destructive habits of mind by recognizing and responding to stimuli in ways that allow individuals to develop more realistic and healthier perceptions, experiences, and responses.

Researchers and clinicians have long identified that it is necessary to take three basic steps to break these negative patterns (Burns, 1980; Ellis & Harper, 1977).

First, it is important to notice when one is actually using them soon after a negative event begins, during a period of anxiety, or when worrying about something. This part of the process requires, of course, some degree of reflection. Then, it is helpful to identify which type of inappropriate reasoning one is using. This procedure involves analyzing one's thoughts to determine whether they fall into one of the problematic categories on the previously mentioned list. Finally, one must counteract the thought by actively correcting it in a way that better corresponds to reality instead of one's imagination or emotions. The more deeply and often one does such work, the more quickly the traps fall apart. These three steps may be represented by the acronym NICC (Notice, Identify, Correct to Counteract), which can be used as a mnemonic to aid memory.

Increasing a Sense of Worthiness

People make mistakes. However, instead of accepting that and trying to deal with errors as realistically as possible, many of us become very good at mobilizing a host of distortions that reduce our sense of worth as a person. Such a tendency is more than unfortunate because we now know that strong negative filters distort reality in ways that make life more difficult to deal with effectively. The repeated use of such cognitive patterns is sure to diminish a sense of one's worth as a person because of the self-fulfilling nature of the process. For instance, the name-calling loop previously mentioned involves a considerable degree of distortion because most people who think of themselves as losers really are not. In fact, they may even be quite good at things. But once such a cognitive anchor is firmly cast, it holds the person to a limited range of possibilities that decreases his or her sense of worth.

Fortunately, we also know it is possible to change such tendencies through the cognitive restructuring process just described. Practicing it long and diligently enough helps people break out of such mental traps, perhaps even at the neuronal level, which is why some people refer to the process as *rewiring* the brain. Most people who advocate this method point out that it is important to write out the steps involved in this change process because these negative mental habits are well ingrained, even automatic. The reasoning here is that writing takes much longer than thinking, so putting pen to paper slows mental processing down enough for one to see how he or she is distorting reality, at least for a moment. That brief period is often enough to allow the individual to temporarily break free of the unhealthy processing loop. Identifying such traps by naming them also helps alter the negative flow of information because names have power, something akin to the way in which having a diagnosis for an illness clears up some of the mystery associated with feeling ill.

Knowing what the real problem is, in this case one's thinking patterns and not the situation alone, allows the individual to replay events to some degree. This action creates a type of second mental chance to deal with what happened more realistically. Taking advantage of this event, in turn, gives the person an opportunity to break free of the distortions and process the event in a healthier fashion. For instance, when someone who consistently calls himself or herself a loser begins to realize that such a reaction is unrealistic, it is easier for him or her to look at new ways of dealing with problematic situations, rather than just continuing to categorize them as more evidence of personal ineptitude.

This approach is backed by very good scientific evidence. In fact, it has been known for decades now that cognitive restructuring or cognitive reframing works at least as well as medications for many forms of anxiety and depression (Durand & Barlow, 2015). Cognitive techniques can also be used to simply help make life better. However, there are two additional factors to keep in mind to avoid making unrealistic expectations that make the method useless. First, these techniques are helpful in reducing suffering, but they are not intended to eliminate all pain: Some events and situations are simply difficult. However, although healthy thinking will not resolve such difficulties overnight, it does reduce unnecessary pain, and realistic thought is usually more effective when dealing with issues than is distorted thought. Second, no one said change is easy. Just as with M, many people have been working on developing poor mental hygiene since childhood. It takes a long time to form these mental habits, so it should not come as a surprise that changing them requires hard work and considerable practice.

In other words, although there is no such thing as a cognitive magic bullet, it should be fairly easy to see how this type of mental rebooting could help people break out of self-esteem traps. In fact, it is possible to illustrate how to do that with another thought activity in Box 4.1a that depicts M during a time when she lost a significant relationship. Afterward, a blank version of the form is given in Box 4.1b for those who wish to try their hand at building positive mental habits related to the worthiness factor of self-esteem or want to include the activity in a journal.

Note that people will usually have a mixture of realistic and distorted thoughts in many situations. In the example, for instance, thinking that things will be different at the end of a relationship is realistic because endings make that happen. Consequently, there is no need to process that thought other than to accept it because it is realistic and allows the brain to treat the thought and accompanying emotions that way.

However, since our cognitive, emotional, and physical systems are designed to respond to what is perceived, we often treat imagined realities as though they are real. For example, most people tense up in a scary movie even though they know nothing dangerous is going to happen. In other words, if one believes that he or she is a loser and will never be loved again, then the brain reacts to the imagined future as though it were real. Such programming may bias various brain, perceptual, and motivational functions enough to process information in that direction. Consistently being attracted to people who would make poor partners, for example, is one effective way to lose again. The point is that there is more value in spending the cognitive and brain-based energies wasted in running this type of mental program on healthier projects. In other words, we can "NICC" these self-esteem traps in their buds.

Box 4.1a

Thought Activity: Breaking Free of Self-Esteem Worthiness Traps with NICC

A. Begin by identifying a situation, event, or interaction that lessened your sense of worthiness as a person. Briefly describe it here. As an example, we can focus on M's recent break-up with a significant other. She first described the situation by writing, "*My partner left me. We broke up.*"

B. Then, use the following steps to break out of self-esteem traps created by faulty patterns.

Step 1: Notice	Step 2: Identify	Step 3: Correct to Counteract
negative thoughts you have about what happened.	the traps unrealistic thoughts created by using the list.	the problematic thoughts to make them more accurate by writing out realistic alternatives.
a. "*I am such a loser.*"	a. *Labeling*	a. "*This loss makes me sad. Sadness is a realistic response and it usually passes with time. Better to be sad than a loser!*"
b. "*No one will ever love me again.*"	b. *Overgeneralizing*	b. "*Who knows what the future will bring? After all, there are lots of fish in the sea.*"

C. Focus on the change in thinking and feeling that occurs at the end of the process: Cognitive restructuring will not make realistic unpleasant feelings, such as sadness in this case, disappear. However, sadness is far better and more realistic than depression or despair because sadness is a normal response to loss and usually passes with time. Thinking realistically reduces distorted perceptions, thoughts, and behaviors, thereby decreasing an unnecessary loss of worthiness and suffering. Remember, the key to the success of this worthiness tool is practice.

Fortunately, noticing the negative thoughts in real time, identifying their actual nature, and then counteracting their effect by correcting them in writing so that they are more realistic all help to disarm self-esteem traps that detract from a realistic and healthy sense of self. Each time someone breaks free of such a snare, even if only momentarily, he or she avoids an unnecessary loss of worth, which in itself is worthwhile. The more often one manages to do that, the more

Box 4.1b

Thought Activity: Breaking Free of Self-Esteem Worthiness Traps with NICC

A. Begin by identifying a situation, event, or interaction that lessened your sense of worthiness as a person. Briefly describe it here:

_____

_____

B. Then use the following steps to break out of any self-esteem traps created by faulty patterns.

Step 1: Notice	Step 2: Identify	Step 3: Correct to Counteract
negative thoughts you have about what happened.	the traps unrealistic thoughts created by using the list.	the problematic thoughts to make them more accurate by writing out realistic alternatives.
a.	a.	a.
b.	b.	b.
c.	c.	c.
d.	d.	d.

C. Finally, focus on the change that occurs at the end of the process. People who do so usually find that things are not as bad as they thought and that a more realistic view reduces an unnecessary loss of worthiness or suffering. Remember, the key to this worthiness tool is practice.

Source: Modified from Mruk C. (2013). *Self-Esteem and positive psychology: Research, theory and practice* (4th ed.). New York, Springer Publishing Company.

stable and worthwhile his or her sense of self becomes, which is helpful when facing a future setback, disappointment, or failure. Once the new habit is sufficiently strengthened, the additional sense of worth should increase the strength of self-esteem's expansion function. When that happens, the process of increasing one's sense of worth in a realistic fashion also tends to facilitate more positive self-experiences and may even trigger the upward cycle associated with positive emotions. In short, it is important to know that people are far from powerless when it comes to changing poor habits of mind.

BREAKING FREE OF COMPETENCE-BASED SELF-ESTEEM TRAPS

For those of us who advocate the two-factor approach, another well-supported method of increasing self-esteem focuses on competence. This component is much more behavioral than emotional, which means learning how to do something better, in this case solving problems, is the way to proceed. Although problem-solving involves a number of mental processes, such as reasoning and self-efficacy, merely thinking in a realistic or positive way is not enough to effectively deal with the challenges of living. As I've stated several times now, authentic self-esteem is earned, not given. Otherwise, one could simply "think and grow rich," as the old saying goes, and most people know that does not happen very often.

Competence, of course, involves doing rather than thinking, so this factor can only be increased by learning how to better deal with challenges, both small and large. Fortunately, social scientists now know something about this process as well. Once again, there are many methods available designed to help people solve problems more effectively and in ways that increase competence. The solution-focused approach I happen to favor is based on work started decades ago and continues to be refined today because evidence shows time and time again that it does, indeed, work (D'Zurilla & Goldfried, 1971). The basic method consists of four relatively simple steps: stating the problem, coming up with solutions, evaluating the consequences of those solutions, and developing a plan of action.

Step 1: State the Problem

The first step involves stating the problem, which may sound simple but often is not. For example, most of us have had the experience of starting to fix something that needed attention and then suddenly realizing half way through the process that we were actually trying to solve the wrong problem right from the beginning. I, for one, cannot even count the number of times I've experienced this difficulty when doing relatively simple jobs like home repairs, because I always seem to make several trips to the hardware store before this type of insight finally occurs and I can get the job done. The point is that it is important to take some time to think about what the difficulty actually is before leaping into action.

Also important to keep in mind, especially for many men, is that there is real value in attending to one's feelings when thinking about problems. My experience as a clinician, and some research from social psychology, support the notion that gender can be a factor to consider when it comes to looking for problems. Perhaps because women tend to be better socialized to pay attention to feelings than are many men, often women seem to recognize problems earlier, especially interpersonal ones. The value of early identification is, of course, that small problems are easier to address than large ones. Consequently, paying attention to feelings this way can be beneficial. In other words, if something feels like a problem, it probably already is one. Since feelings often precede conscious analysis, it is wise to learn how to pay close attention to one's feelings whenever possible.

Step 2: Brainstorm Potential Solutions

Next, it is important to do some brainstorming or to at least generate a number of possible solutions to the problem. The trick here is to avoid judging them, as doing so restricts one's ability to be creative or to consider different approaches, especially thinking out of the box, which is often most helpful when solving problems. Rather, simply list possible alternatives that come to mind after some reflection on the problem—without evaluating them.

Step 3: Evaluate Potential Solutions

The third step is to evaluate the solutions generated in the second. The recommended approach is to take the time to identify and reflect on the consequences that are likely to occur with each possible solution, one after another. Writing them down is a good idea for the reasons discussed earlier. After doing so, it is then possible to select the one that is *best* and use it in the next and final step.

I put the term *best* in italics for a very important reason. Often people know what the ideal, most rational, or clearly superior solution to a problem is. Sometimes, however, they are not willing to implement that choice because it requires too much work or may be too disruptive to other parts of their lives to be a practical alternative. For example, the *best* way to deal with a nicotine addiction is to simply stop using the substance—period. However, for most people, that solution is too difficult to implement. Instead, cutting down, wearing a patch, or getting into treatment is likely to be better, even though the addiction persists for a time. So for me, *best* means the most desirable and realistic alternative because it is the one that is most likely to actually get done. In short, the best solution is usually the one that a given individual is willing to take responsibility for and to put into action.

Step 4: Develop a Plan

Finally comes the last step, which is to develop a plan of action. This one also requires some thought. Many people will select a solution that they can live with but then create a plan that is either unrealistic or that involves taking very large steps to complete, as in the example concerning addiction. Either of these common mistakes may doom the plan to failure. Instead, it is very important to make sure the plan is feasible, which often means creating a series of small, realistic, clear, and, above all, approach-oriented steps. Remember, we saw in chapter 2 that setting approach goals involves forming well-conceived and doable steps to increase one's chances of reaching a desirable goal or destination.

Learning how to solve problems better is just like learning anything else: One starts out poorly but slowly progresses over time, providing one keeps at it. After all, making one trip to the gym to lose weight may only result in being tired and, perhaps, sore the next day. It is coming back on a regular basis or practice that makes exercise work. Why should learning to solve problems better be any different? The thought activity for problem-solving presented in Box 4.2a uses the example of M

Box 4.2a

THOUGHT ACTIVITY: INCREASING COMPETENCE WITH PROBLEM-SOLVING SKILLS

Basic four-step problem-solving method: Move through the steps and be sure to detail the plan.

Step 1: Problem	**Step 2: Solutions**	**Step 3: Consequences**
a. I need a new job.	*a. Do nothing.*	*a. No change is likely this way.*
	b. Read job ads.	*b. I could get lucky this way.*
	c. Ask friends.	*c. I could get lucky this way.*
	d. Seek professional help.	*d. Professionals are trained to help and should have better resources than I have on my own.*

Step 4: (Best) Plan

a. *I am willing to do solution d because it seems most realistic, and it gets people off my back.*

b. *The first goal, then, is to find a professional I can afford and get to in person. This part of the plan involves doing some research like an Internet search or talking with a career counselor at a local educational, training, or unemployment agency.*

c. *The next task is to set up an interview with the career counselor. That will at least get me out of the house, which should make me feel better, and get me help in developing a detailed and realistic plan of action I could actually do.*

d. *During the interview, I will be sure to ask about a scholarship or financial support. After all, I did do OK in school, and I do have a good work record. Of course, if I had a drug problem I'd probably have to work on that issue to get a job, but I am fortunate to not have one.*

Box 4.2b

THOUGHT ACTIVITY: INCREASING COMPETENCE
WITH PROBLEM-SOLVING SKILLS

Basic four-step problem-solving method: Move through the steps and be sure to detail the plan.

Step 1: Problem   **Step 2: Solutions**   **Step 3: Consequences**

a.   a.   a.

                             b.   b.

                             c.   c.

                             d.   d.

Step 4: (Best) Plan

   a. _____

   b. _____

   c. _____

   d. (etc.) _____

Source: Modified from Mruk, C. (2013). *Self-Esteem and positive psychology: Research, theory, and practice* (4th ed.). New York, Springer Publishing Company.

losing her job, which occurred at one point in treatment. A blank version of the form follows in in Box 4.2b for those who wish to try it out themselves.

DEVELOPING A POSITIVE SELF-ESTEEM ACTION PLAN

Notice that one of the methods for increasing authentic self-esteem involves understanding ways to reduce thinking patterns that lessen one's sense of worth and that the other one focuses on the second factor necessary for authentic self-esteem, namely, increasing competence. Since authentic self-esteem involves a relationship between these two factors, it is necessary to bring them together, something that may best be done slowly but regularly to avoid being discouraged by that fact that change takes time. One way of doing that is through what I call a *self-esteem action plan* (Mruk, 2013a).

This method has been tested with both clinical and everyday populations and can be adapted to the goals of this book through another thought experiment. The three-step plan begins with examining the six domains of life in which self-esteem plays a role. Next, the individual may select a particular area affecting self-esteem in which improvement is desired. Finally, one uses the two techniques previously described, namely, cognitive restructuring to cut down on the erosion of worthiness caused by cognitive self-esteem traps and problem-solving to develop the skills needed to break free of traps that limit competence in a given area.

Step 1: Assessing/Examining One's Self-Esteem

Of course, no two people ever score quite the same on any assessment of self-esteem because each individual values different areas of life within the six domains that contribute to the development of self-esteem. That is why it is best to do what may be called an *individualized assessment* (Fischer, 1986) of self-esteem. For example, I now care more about physical ability than appearance because I am aging and want to do the things that make life enjoyable for as long as possible. That does not mean that appearance is unimportant—thinking about losing hair, or other things, is not pleasant. However, if I had to choose between a hair transplant and developing a plan to stay in reasonable physical shape for as long as possible, it is easy to identify which one is more likely to increase or at least maintain a sense of competence. Still, someone else might see physical appearance as more valuable and work on improving it instead through such things as exercising, fashion consulting, and so on to increase one's feeling of worth through genuinely positive feedback from others.

To illustrate the concepts of individualized self-esteem assessment and positive action planning based upon it, I will first take M through the process in narrative form. Now in her early 30s, M is of average but pleasant appearance, continues to be articulate, has one child, is currently involved with someone, and is just starting to be successful in regard to a new line of work. Unfortunately, she still has a problem with appropriately asserting herself, and it continues to negatively affect the quality of her work. Since life is seldom limited to a single problem, it is learned that M is also having difficulties maintaining a satisfying relationship that affirms her worth as a person. Instead, she repeatedly chooses partners who become unfaithful. As a result, M thinks that having more authentic self-esteem would help in both areas and wonders how to get there.

One way to begin is to take a test that assesses one's general or overall self-esteem, which is known as *trait self-esteem* in the field (see Box 4.3a). An even better instrument would reveal an individual's particular self-esteem strengths and weaknesses as well. One very good professional tool I used with clients is the Multidimensional Self-Esteem Inventory (O'Brien & Epstein, 1988). However, it requires a professional to administer, score, and interpret, so it cannot be offered here. While I encourage clinicians to consider that approach, another one is to ask an individual to seriously reflect on, in a structured way, the six domains described earlier and then select the one that seems most relevant to life right now. Such results might look like M's self-assessment which is presented next (see Box 4.3b). Even if one does

Box 4.3a

THOUGHT ACTIVITY: SELF-DIRECTED SELF-ESTEEM ASSESSMENT FORMAT

A. **Worthiness Domains (for M)**

1. **Being Connected:** This domain involves the quality of relationships in your life as that has been shown to be connected to both self-esteem and happiness in general.
   A. Greatest Strength: *Being faithful in relationships.*
   B. Area to Work On: *Picking partners who feel the same way about fidelity.*
   C. Importance to M: *Very high.*

2. **Physical Attractiveness:** This item concerns how important you think physical attractiveness is for you in general.
   A. Greatest Strength: *I look younger than I am.*
   B. Area to Work On: *I could afford to lose some weight.*
   C. Importance to M: *Average, nothing in particular to worry about or change.*

3. **Morality and Virtue:** This dimension focuses on a very important aspect of positive self-regulation: the ability to comport yourself in a way that is virtuous or worthy of a fully functioning person.
   A. Greatest Strength: *I am dependable and tend to be generous.*
   B. Area to Work On: *Often I react to negative things in immature or too emotional ways.*
   C. Importance to M: *Average. We can all stand some improvement in this area!*

B. **Competence Domains (for M)**

1. **Problem-Solving Abilities:** This item deals with your ability to function well at work, manage finances, run a home, and deal with the tasks of living.
   A. Greatest Strength: *Self-motivated, I work well alone or in small groups.*
   B. Area to Work On: *I just don't seem to be able to assert myself appropriately at work.*
   C. Importance to M: *Very high. Lifelong issue.*

2. **Autonomy and Control:** This domain concerns the degree to which you are able to have a voice in regard to situations or environments, including social ones, in your life.
   A. Greatest Strength: *People tend to take my input seriously most of the time.*
   B. Area to Work On: *Learning how to better control anxiety when I try to assert myself.*
   C. Importance to M: *High. The anxiety about asserting myself is limiting my ability to direct or influence my life.*

3. **Physical Integrity:** This dimension involves the extent to which your physical potentials and limitations affect your ability to do the things you want or need to do.
   A. Greatest Strength: *In pretty good shape right now; could be better.*
   B. Area to Work on: *Nothing to be concerned about right now.*
   C. Importance to M: *Low. Things are OK now.*

Box 4.3b

THOUGHT ACTIVITY: SELF-DIRECTED SELF-ESTEEM ASSESSMENT FORMAT

A. Worthiness Domains

1. Being Connected: This domain involves the quality of relationships in your life as that has been shown to be connected to both self-esteem and happiness in general.

A. Greatest Strength: _____

B. Area to Work On: _____

C. Importance: _____

2. Physical Attractiveness: This item concerns how important you think physical attractiveness is for you in general.

A. Greatest Strength: _____

B. Area to Work On: _____

C. Importance: _____

3. Morality and Virtue: This dimension focuses on a very important aspect of positive self-regulation: the ability to comport yourself in a way that is virtuous or worthy of a fully functioning person.

A. Greatest Strength: _____

B. Area to Work On: _____

C. Importance: _____

B. Competence Domains

1. Problem-Solving Abilities: This item deals with your ability to function well at work, manage finances, run a home, and deal with the tasks of living.

A. Greatest Strength: _____

B. Area to Work On: _____

C. Importance: _____

2. **Autonomy and Control:** This domain concerns the degree to which you have the ability to have a voice in regard to situations or environments, including social ones, in your life.

   A. Greatest Strength: _____

   B. Area to Work On: _____

   C. Importance: _____

3. **Physical Integrity:** This dimension involves the extent to which your physical potentials and limitations affect your ability to do the things you want or need to do.

   A. Greatest Strength: _____

   B. Area to Work On: _____

   C. Importance: _____

---

not use the form to develop a self-esteem action plan, its categories are still worth reflecting upon.

Step 2: Selecting an Issue

Most people with self-esteem issues, including those with medium self-esteem, want to do better in life. The aim of a self-esteem action plan is consistent with this basic human motivation in a very straightforward way: It simply involves using the results of the assessment to identify a self-esteem issue to take through the problem-solving process just presented. In other words, it is possible to examine one's own self-esteem issues in a given domain, identify one area to work on, and then set up a realistic action plan aimed at enhancing self-esteem in that part of one's life. In M's case, for example, it is clear that one difficulty is in the area of worthiness (being connected to others) and two others are connected to competence (problem-solving and autonomy/control).

Not surprisingly, it also happens that sometimes people have such low or defensive self-esteem that they cannot tolerate working with weaknesses. In this case, it would be far better to target a self-esteem strength the person possesses and then build a plan around it to increase competence or worth. As growth in this area occurs, it could help the individual feel more able to deal with a self-esteem problem area next. Either way, the psychology of self-regulation demonstrated that it is a limited ability, so it is probably best to focus on one self-improvement project at a time. Since competence-related issues show up twice and worthiness only once for M, it may be best to settle on developing skills relating to assertiveness, especially since that issue is now standing in the way of self-expansion in the workplace, thereby limiting her life in a number of important ways.

It is important to remember that according to research on self-regulation, people have a better chance of succeeding at something when they adopt approach goals rather than avoidance goals. For example, instead of fretting about a lack of assertiveness, a positive plan might involve setting up two approach-oriented goals. One could be making a systematic effort to reduce unrealistic cognitive thinking patterns or habits of mind that make one feel unworthy of the right to stand up for oneself. The other might involve learning how to assert oneself appropriately in certain situations without becoming aggressive or obnoxious.

Step 3: Using the Plan

Since even thinking about self-assertion seems to create anxiety, M decided to start identifying the types of thoughts that arise at these times to examine whether they included distortions. For example, after speaking up for herself M would typically think something like, "I sounded dumb," which is the name-calling error we identified previously. She happened to find that keeping a journal or log of such things helped to identify the most common distortions she tended to make. It also became clear to M that writing them out seemed to slow down the process enough for her to see the errors in these ways of thinking and correct them using the NICC approach. For instance, a more realistic correction of the distortions found in the previous example might be, "No one said I was dumb, and there was no other evidence for that, so that distortion needs to be replaced with a more realistic thought." In this way, she prevented undermining her sense of worth because of self-demeaning thinking patterns.

Similarly, after working her difficulties through the problem-solving method, M decided to take the next step and do the work necessary to increase competence in this domain. She signed up for a very basic assertiveness training seminar at an adult education center where all she had to do was listen to a presentation on one's right to be more assertive. After that step was successfully completed, M signed up for an assertiveness training class at the center. About half way through the program, she even volunteered to co-lead some of the sessions to acquire greater competency in the area. Eventually, M's success with these smaller steps enabled her to ask for a promotion and raise at work, something she would never have done more than dream about before.

Although the anxiety associated with being assertive never completely went away for M, she became quite able to assert herself when necessary. And if a mistake happened to occur, it did not seem bothersome for long, providing she remembered to restructure unrealistic cognitions by correcting and counteracting them when needed. As a result, cognitive distortions concerning worthiness decreased, success in a meaningful domain of life verified an increase in competence, and authentic self-esteem went up. Accordingly, M's ability to see possibilities broadened, the motivation to explore them became more appealing, and the courage to take appropriate risks increased sufficiently enough to actualize new possibilities with reasonable frequency, just as the self-expansion function of self-esteem would predict. If done often enough, these changes could also trigger an upward cycle of positive emotion, experience, and behavior in related areas of life as well.

Note that for some people, the relationship issue concerning being affirmed as an individual who is worthy of fidelity from a partner as previously mentioned might be more important to work on at first. If M selected this issue instead of the other, it could mean that her career might suffer for a while longer, but developing a worthiness-oriented self-esteem project often improves well-being too. In her particular case, M suffers from a problem with worth that involves a lack of opportunity to interact with others who share similar values concerning the type of honor or respect that is associated with fidelity. To form a self-esteem action plan around this type of issue, she might benefit from changing her dating preferences, which could mean learning to better tolerate loneliness until she meets the "right" person. Regardless of whether a competence or worthiness-based self-esteem issue is chosen, the process for increasing authentic self-esteem is the same: It involves identifying and correcting cognitive self-esteem traps, running the issue through the problem-solving method until one determines a best (most realistic) plan of action, and implementing the steps one by one until new and healthier self-esteem behaviors emerge.

INCREASING SELF-ESTEEM BY USING SELF-ESTEEM MOMENTS

Whether the issue is competence or worthiness, it should be noted that another important benefit comes with mustering the courage to face life's challenges in more authentic ways: The individual starts to have more positive self-esteem moments in the domains of life that give rise to problematic self-esteem in the first place. If these new and more positive self-esteem moments are significant enough, or even if only small positive self-esteem moments occur often enough, then deeper changes may occur. In other words, it is possible to heal problematic self-esteem themes. Given sufficient time and effort, this positive process is strong enough to help an individual shift from a state of low or defensive self-esteem to one of medium self-esteem or to move from medium self-esteem to authentic self-esteem, depending on which type and level the person began with initially.

For the most part, increasing authentic self-esteem in a slow but steady fashion is best because it can be planned and because inevitable setbacks can be dealt with more easily. This method also allows for the benefit of practice, which can help overwrite older habits that detract from competence, worthiness, or both. In addition, some people simply need to go slowly, especially if they have deep-seated worthiness problems. For example, I knew one woman who was interested in joining a self-esteem therapy group I was running but then found that she could not even attend the first meeting. When I asked why, she said, "I don't think I am worthy of feeling worthy."

Research on changing self-esteem suggests taking very small steps in this type of situation. In the clinical setting, for instance, self-esteem therapists report that clients grow more if the therapist offers mild positive feedback in slow but consistent doses over time (Bednar, Wells, & Peterson, 1989). Remember, very low self-esteem is also very stable self-esteem, so a gradual process might be more effective than a dramatic one for some people. In fact, the previously cited work indicated that too much positive feedback at one time may even have a negative impact on therapy for those with very low self-esteem, just as my own experience with the woman who felt unworthy of therapy indicates. Similarly, those with defensive self-esteem often need to go slow because it can take them a while to realize that people who are trying to help are not interested in humiliating, belittling, or otherwise threatening them, even though such an individual might feel like that is happening in therapy at times.

Self-esteem action plans help because they are ways of increasing the chances one has of experiencing more positive self-esteem moments in an area of life that is tied to one's identity. The idea, of course, is to increase authentic self-esteem incrementally by helping people make better decisions when they are challenged in a way that requires showing some degree of competence or worthiness in everyday life. In addition, gradually filling the bucket by earning self-esteem through one's own actions in these ways may actually shift one's running total of competence and worthiness from one type or level to another. The reason I call this approach to increasing authentic self-esteem an *action plan* is because it is possible to deliberately create a series of steps that help people reach such an approach-oriented goal.

The other way of using self-esteem moments to increase authentic self-esteem is more difficult to build into a plan because it only occurs when a person is challenged by a situation that activates a problematic self-esteem theme in the here and now of a person's actual life. These crossroads of self-esteem, which were first presented in chapter 3, are potentially valuable because they always involve both competence and worthiness. They are the self-esteem moments that are powerful enough to put a significant portion of one's identity at-stake. This existential crisis occurs, it will be recalled, because it involves facing a challenge of living on two levels. One of them usually seems fairly obvious, and the other is not because it concerns troublesome self-esteem themes rooted in one's personal history or character. This dimension of the challenge is what makes it a *crossroad*, a word used to describe the fact that which particular path one takes at this time will have a strong positive or negative effect on his or her basic, general, or trait self-esteem.

These self-esteem moments have been studied clinically and found to be turning points in regard to the development of self-esteem no matter what a person's age or circumstances might happen to be (Bednar, Wells, & Peterson, 1989; Jackson, 1984; Mruk, 2013a). Since this book is more concerned with everyday life rather than research, it is appropriate to focus on the practical implications of such work. First, these very powerful self-esteem moments are often, (but not always), triggered by a fairly ordinary event. For example, some clients have told me how seemingly simple things, such as visiting a friend in a hospital, feeling lonely at a party, or even just speaking up to a bully, soon led to a crossroad of competence and worthiness.

In the first case, a young man wished to visit a friend who was ill and in the hospital, which is a perfectly reasonable desire. However, when he learned that she was on the 15th floor, he suddenly found himself facing a nearly paralyzing long-term fear of elevators to do the right thing, as there was no other way to get to her room. Near the end of a party, a woman who had never learned that she was worthy without being with a partner found herself beginning to struggle with a very familiar compromising sexual possibility yet again in order to avoid being alone that night when everyone left. And another person found himself having to either succumb to the unrealistic demands of a boss who stirred up unpleasant memories of being bullied by authority figures most of his life or confront both the individual and the problematic self-esteem past at the same time.

What all of these seemingly ordinary challenges had in common that made them so significant for self-esteem is not the immediate or surface conflict, though they were certainly unpleasant. The difficult part was that for each individual, the conflict suddenly invoked the need to face a personally problematic self-esteem theme. The problem is that doing that which is just and right is relatively easy to figure out but also involves facing a painful personal fear, obstacle, or limitation, which requires a measure of courage where there has been little in the past.

If the individual takes the higher road, then he or she clearly expresses a form of worthiness and simultaneously demonstrates an undeniable degree of competence at dealing with the challenges of living on both levels of the problem. Such a positive response maintains the integrity of one's self, affirms one's identity, and expands possibilities in life in ways that are consistent with the self-enhancement function of self-esteem. On the other hand, failing to acknowledge the full meaning of the situation or taking an easier way out, which usually involves some form of self-deception like denial, blaming, or rationalization leads in the opposite direction. Taking the lower or self-protective road at this self-esteem juncture results in losing individual worth, staying stuck at a lower level of competence, and feeling various negative emotions, such as disappointment, regret, guilt, or even shame, all of which affect self-esteem but in a negative way.

The research on these self-esteem moments indicates that people seem to go through a six-stage process as they live through such crises of self-esteem (Mruk, 2013a). In order, they are:

1. Encountering a problem where one is challenged to do something that is virtuous and in which the just and right choice is clear.
2. Coming to find that the situation activates a problematic self-esteem theme that puts one's identity at stake in terms of competence and worthiness.
3. Struggling with the self-esteem theme by vacillating between an approach goal (doing the right thing) and an avoidance goal (avoiding dealing with the underlying theme).

4. Becoming increasingly aware of how much is at stake and finding the courage to move one step beyond old boundaries in the right direction.
5. Experiencing the positive meaning of the choice and expanding the self as well as possibilities in life.
6. Learning that the choice healed some of the problematic self-esteem theme and significantly increased authentic self-esteem.

The middle portion of the process (steps 3 and 4) seems to be the tipping point in determining whether there will be a positive or negative outcome for self-esteem, so let me describe this part more fully.

After encountering the initial problem, the person becomes aware of the implications his or her decision will have on self-esteem. There are four elements that seem to help people make a healthy or authentic choice, rather than the unhealthy or inauthentic one they historically make at these times. All but the last one involves increasing one's awareness, which is something, it will be recalled, that Kernis (2003) associated with optimal self-esteem and that humanistic psychology considers a part of authenticity in general.

The first factor usually involves acknowledging that part of one's identity is really at stake in this situation, namely one's worth as a person, and that this dimension of the conflict is crucial to accept. The second is realizing that one has faced this situation before, sometimes many times before as in the case of, for example, dealing with an addiction or a personal weakness. The third involves accepting the fact that the behavior one usually uses to deal with this situation does not work and is not likely to be effective this time either.

The fourth point is more difficult to articulate because it involves an intersection between several factors. They include a fear of the present situation and past memories of similar ones that did not end well, the conflict generated by the two functions of self-esteem competing for dominance in the situation with one calling for courage and the other urging safety, and a short supply of time before a decision has to be made. The pivotal moment seems to occur when one's desire to grow exceeds the need to feel safe. At this point, the paradox of self-esteem shifts such that the drive to expand is at least equal to the desire to be safe. Such a development seems to break a chain to the past and momentarily frees the individual to try to become more authentic.

At the point that one's awareness of possibilities begins to broaden, courage becomes a crucial factor. Courage, of course, is a part of life that is not well understood partly because, by definition, it is impossible to predict. But even if the attempt fails, making this type of response still diminishes the power of some old cognitive and behavioral patterns because it adds a new element to the existing self-esteem picture. Being successful, of course, has the additional advantage of increasing one's competence now and in the future when facing similar situations. The result of dealing with such an existential challenge in this fashion is that it always creates some degree of authentic self-esteem.

As indicated earlier, most people have problematic self-esteem themes concerning their competence and/or worth as a person that can become activated in this way. Like the concepts of the repetition compulsion or karma, people are fated to face them again and again until they "feel good by doing good," as the title of this book suggests. The same dynamics mean, of course, that self-esteem, even authentic self-esteem, can be lost in life especially if one turns away from the challenge or attempts to deal with it in a dishonorable or unworthy fashion. Fortunately, however, each person described in this chapter took the higher road: A man comforted his friend, a person respected her own worth that evening, and someone broke a chain of submission that used to only result in loss or self-loathing.

5

Self-Esteem and Individual Well-Being

Chapter 2 considered the relationship between authentic self-esteem and well-being in terms of self-regulation and control. Since both of the major functions of self-esteem are tied to those processes, it is reasonable to anticipate finding the relationship between self-esteem and well-being to also exist on two fronts of life.

On one hand, observing what happens when a crucial component is missing is often a good way to learn about its value, just as being ill usually teaches a lot about the importance of health. It was pointed out in chapter 1, for example, that there is general agreement that healthy self-esteem is desirable because it buffers people from stress, anxiety, and a host of negative phenomena (Leary & MacDonald, 2003). Those who work with mental illness have first-hand experience with this connection between self-esteem and well-being or, more properly, a lack of it because the benefits that come with competence and worthiness working together are strongly made known by their absence.

Similarly, most people find that it is difficult to be around individuals for any length of time who have even moderate degrees of unstable self-esteem because of their tendency to become defensive, rigid, critical, or interpersonally aggressive, especially when stressed. Finally, that fact that self-esteem is tied to at least six important domains of existence that run across the entire life cycle in one way or another means that the self-protective function of self-esteem covers a lot of territory related to well-being. Few would want to be without the shield that healthy self-esteem provides for long, which is why social scientists have studied the self-protective function the most.

On the other hand, humanistic psychology has been concerned with the growth-related function of self-esteem for over a half-century, and now positive psychology is becoming increasingly interested in this dimension of self-esteem too (Churchill & Mruk, 2014; Mruk, 2013a). Such a development is fortunate because this dimension of self-esteem is more directly connected to mental health and well-being. Moreover, the enhancing function of self-esteem is also relevant to everyone, not just those who suffer from its lack. For example, even people with medium or normal self-esteem who are faring reasonably well in life can benefit from better understanding the benefits of self-esteem and how to enhance it. Consequently, this chapter focuses on the positive connections between authentic self-esteem and well-being, especially as they occur in everyday life.

SELF-ESTEEM, MENTAL HEALTH, AND WELL-BEING

Unlike much of traditional clinical psychology, both humanistic and positive psychology are more concerned with mental health, although they still focus on helping people in need, of course. In social work, this emphasis on well-being is sometimes known as the *strength approach* because it focuses more on what people can do to make their lives better than on what they lack or cannot do (Murphy & Dillon, 2011). These positive approaches to understanding and changing behavior are more comprehensive because they consider the whole person, not just what is wrong with him or her. Emphasizing what is possible and not what is problematic is consistent with an interest in understanding how the expansion function of self-esteem connects it to well-being. Consequently, it is best to begin this exploration by examining material on mental health instead of illness.

Two models of mental health are especially useful for understanding the connections between self-esteem, mental health, and well-being. Corey Keyes (2002) presented one that is based on the concept of whether one is *flourishing* as a human being, which is to say living a satisfying and meaningful life. Mental health is based on two factors according to this view. One is the absence of symptoms associated with a significant degree of unhappiness, personal or inter-personal difficulties, and mental health issues. The other is the degree to which one experiences happiness and a sense of satisfaction on a regular basis as indicated by such things as positive experiences, healthy interpersonal connections, and a sense of purpose or meaning in life.

People who are characterized by low levels of mental illness and high degrees of well-being are said to be flourishing. They constitute about 17% of the population according to various adherents of this model and have positive levels of mental health. Conversely, those who live with a high number of symptoms and low degrees of well-being, another 17% or so, are considered to be at the opposite end of the mental health continuum. They are referred to as *suffering* because they often struggle with life.

Finally, this model characterizes those who experience low symptoms and low well-being, or low symptoms and minimal well-being, as *languishing*. This state certainly allows one to function reasonably well, but it also means that things could be much better. The group also constitutes the majority of the population. For example, people with medium self-esteem would be found here because their levels of competence and worthiness mean that they are not floundering.

However, this state does make a difference because it means they are in a good position to move toward authentic self-esteem and greater well-being.

Authentic self-esteem certainly would play a significant role in this approach to mental health because, in addition to reducing the impact of stress, competence and worthiness help people more effectively deal with the trials and tribulations of living in more positive and productive ways. The balance between the two factors would also make engaging in destructive behaviors, such as excessive use of substances, unhealthy life styles, and poor relational choices, less likely and thereby reduce the likelihood of serious symptomology. In addition, the healthy emotions associated with "feeling good by doing good," to paraphrase Milton once again, should result in more of the positive experiences and higher degrees of satisfaction associated with flourishing. Unfortunately, however, the flourishing model does not delineate the particular ways in which authentic self-esteem is connected to well-being, so another one must be selected.

Fortunately, these links are more apparent in the model of mental health offered by Carol Ryff and Burton Singer (1998). This view, called *psychological well-being*, involves doing reasonably well in three areas of life, namely, emotionally, psychologically, and socially. The first involves healthy affective functioning, which is indicated by such things as experiencing more positive feelings and states than negative ones, being more happy than unhappy, and having higher degrees of satisfaction with life in general. Positive emotions, it should be recalled, are associated with the self-expansion function of self-esteem because it feels good to effectively resolve challenges, because breaking through limitations does broaden one's perspective, and because the action tendency of trying something new helps one to grow personally as well as interpersonally. This connection between authentic self-esteem and well-being was first made in chapter 2 and fulfills the initial requirement of the model.

The second and more psychological dimension of mental health and well-being described by Ryff and Singer (1998) involves functioning reasonably well in six identifiable ways. They are self-acceptance, personal growth, purpose in life, environmental mastery, autonomy, and positive relations with others. Let us examine each such characteristic in terms of the work we have seen on authentic self-esteem so far in order to better establish and appreciate its connections to mental health and individual well-being.

The connection between self-esteem and acceptance is clearly evidenced by the fact that acceptance is a major source of self-esteem, one that is crucial for developing and maintaining a sense of worthiness as a person. Next, it was shown that the expansion function of self-esteem is a key element in the personal growth process: One's ability to develop is very limited without the capacity to take appropriate risks, which is fostered by healthy self-esteem. Continuing onward, purpose in life is something that we did not explore so far, so it remains to be addressed in this chapter. However, it is easy to see the relationship between the next dimension of mental health, well-being, and authentic self-esteem because environmental mastery requires competence. Competence, it will be recalled, has been a steady theme in this book. Autonomy is also a familiar topic as it was explored as a basic domain of life and reflects a basic source of self-esteem, namely, power or influence. Finally, the connection between self-esteem and positive relationships was touched on concerning the correlation between self-esteem, happiness, and marriage, although the next chapter deals with self-esteem, relationships, and well-being in more detail.

The third and last part of Ryff and Singer's (1998) view of mental health concerns social well-being. This dimension of mental health has four related components, namely, social acceptance, social contributions, social integration, and social coherence. The connection between social acceptance, self-esteem, and mental health or well-being is easy to see in regard to worthiness in the two-factor model. Epstein's work on self-esteem in relationships, for example, showed this connection quite clearly when he found that being accepted by another person (or group of people) increases self-esteem, while being rejected has the opposite effect. Social contributions involve making valued contributions to one's imme-diate group, something that is easily seen in the type of virtue associated with self-esteem that, for instance, comes after doing something to help another. Social integration functions in a way that is similar to the role self-esteem plays in evo-lutionary thinking in that self-esteem helps regulate personal and interpersonal behaviors, usually in prosocial ways.

In sum, it is fair to say that authentic self-esteem is connected to mental health and well-being in all of the ways the model requires except in regard to having purpose in life and social coherence. Developing a sense of purpose in life is a personal matter, and since this chapter deals with individual well-being, we will focus on this link here. Since social coherence comes from feeling connected to the larger human community, or to humanity in general, that final connection will be explored in chapter 6.

First, however, it is necessary to appreciate two more things because they act as general rules for governing the connections between authentic self-esteem, mental health, and well-being. One is the fact that feelings, personality, and relationships all work together. This phenomenon means that all the components in the model are connected to and affect each other to produce states of being, namely, well-being or the lack of it. The other is that there is so much variation in personality, abilities, and interests from person to person that it would be a mistake to think that an individual must flourish in each part of all three dimensions of this model to experience good mental health. Rather, just good enough development really is just good enough. In other words, as long as there is an absence of illness or psy-chopathology, it is only necessary to be doing reasonably well in most of the areas previously mentioned for one to experience a meaningful degree of mental health and psychological well-being. It is even possible that some people may reach such an approach-oriented goal by doing very well in a few areas.

AUTHENTIC SELF-ESTEEM AND HAPPINESS

It might be tempting to lump happiness and satisfaction with life together be-cause they have many similarities and because they are positive states related to self-esteem. For example, both can involve an abundance of positive feelings and experiences that make life more pleasant and enjoyable. However, there are some important differences that clearly distinguish the two forms of well-being, so they must be considered separately. More to the point, it is very possible to be satisfied with one's life even though it is not a pleasant one. Indeed, many great figures in history have led very difficult lives. People like Abraham Lincoln, Martin Luther King Jr., and Mother Teresa show time and time again that dedicating oneself to a meaningful goal often means hardship and sometimes sacrifices of the highest order, including life itself. Satisfaction with life has more to do with its meaning or purpose, while happiness is usually more hedonic or pleasure centered. Since happiness is simpler, it is best to begin by considering the relationship between happiness and self-esteem before doing the same with satisfaction of life or purpose.

One way to explore the relationship between authentic self-esteem and happiness is to ask an illustrative question: "Which of the following is correct? Happy people (a) have happier relationships than others; (b) make more money than others; (c) tend to be healthier than others; (d) tolerate stress better than others; or (e) may live longer than others." Many, if not most researchers who study happiness, indicate that the correct answer would be "all of the above" (Diener & Diener, 1995). Although it is not necessary to go into all of the research behind each item, it is useful to quickly identify some of the links between happiness and self-esteem brought up by this question.

Grounds for the first possible answer are found in the reciprocal relationship between self-esteem and interpersonal phenomena in chapter 2: In survey after survey on happiness, happy people report more happy relationships, especially marriages, more than anyone else. Money is next, and this area of life also involves reciprocal connections with self-esteem and happiness. For example, those who study leadership, the ability to work in groups, and assertiveness find that self-esteem can affect performance. Performance, as we know, is often related to such things as salary, promotion, and the various socioeconomic possibilities that come with them (Stinson, Logel, Zanna, Holmes, & Cameron, 2008).

The third possibility, health, is supported by several studies indicating that people with low self-esteem tend to make poorer health-related decisions when it comes to taking care of themselves than do those with higher levels of self-esteem. For instance, episodes of drinking, abusing drugs, or eating excessively have been found to increase during stressful personal and interpersonal periods for those who suffer low self-esteem compared to people with high self-esteem. It is well known, of course, that such behaviors contribute to various types of physical health problems, such as high blood pressure and other cardiovascular conditions, but we also saw that low self-esteem affects mental health (Crocker & Park, 2004; O'Brien, Bartoletti, & Leitzel, 2006).

Next, most people have heard or read about the ways in which stress can contribute to a host of mental, physical, or relational problems so often that there is no reason to elaborate the point: Life without a good buffering system simply makes happiness more difficult to find. Finally, it seems reasonable to think that people who accept and stand up for themselves, both of which are to be expected from someone with authentic self-esteem, have a better chance at living longer than those who do not. In short, while one might argue about the strength of each such connection between self-esteem, happiness, and well-being, at the very least it seems reasonable to say that one would be foolish to ignore these links in the long run of life (Stinson, Logel, Zanna, Holmes, & Cameron, 2008).

General Happiness Factors

Several positive psychologists study happiness, and their findings are worth noting in any discussion concerning this dimension of well-being. For example, Sonja Lyubomirsky (2001) and others indicate that one's general level of happiness is based on three factors. One is called the *happiness set point* and is largely grounded in biology. Some people, it appears, just seem happier than others most of the time. Such dispositional happiness has to do with biological factors concerning temperament, activity level, need for stimulation, neurotransmitter functioning, and the like, all of which are primarily genetic in nature.

Environmental influences are another set of factors. This dimension of happiness is probably most clearly seen in terms of economics. Basically, those who struggle to survive have fewer opportunities to enjoy positive experiences because they must devote so much of their energy to fulfilling basic needs for food, housing, and so forth (although positive experiences do occur under such conditions). Surprisingly enough, however, the majority of researchers who work on happiness have determined that of the three factors, the environmental portion of individual happiness accounts for the smallest percentage of this dimension of well-being. After all, certain poorer nations often report higher levels of happiness than some affluent ones in international studies (Helliwell, Layard, & Sachs, 2016).

The third and most important set of influences affecting happiness are called *volitional factors*, which is a more scientific way of talking about the variables that we can control, or at least influence, as individuals. For example, earlier we saw that having influence, which certainly is volitional, is a source of self-esteem. Since these are the factors that one can do the most about, this personal connection between self-esteem and happiness warrants further attention.

Much of the research on volitional factors involves examining positive feelings, experiences, and behaviors people have because these phenomena are relatively easy to identify and study, unlike work on satisfaction and purpose or meaning in life. Humanistic and positive psychologists, for instance, have found that *flow* is one such state and that it is an indication of at least some degree of well-being (Csikszentmihályi, 1990). This term is used to describe what happens for people when they become engaged in activity in which they find themselves so involved that they lose track of time and a sense of self. These tasks always involve facing a certain type of challenge or series of them. The challenge (or series of them) must be great enough to require high degrees of concentration and engagement to meet its demands but not so much so as to make success extraordinarily difficult. In other words, the activity must be interesting, motivating, and just beyond one's current ability so that keeping up with the task or challenge is a moment-by-moment process demanding high levels of attention, concentration, and effort even if it is only intellectual. Another way of saying the same thing is that these challenges allow us to authentically "be all we can be" in a particular domain of life at a specific point in time.

Research on flow has been done on many activities including bicycling, chess, mountain climbing, various crafts, and even work. This material reveals two important things about such states that are important in regard to self-esteem. One is that the particular activity is usually of intrinsic interest or value for it to be able to generate flow. This factor means, of course, that people find flow in very different ways: Indeed, one person's flow might be another's tedium. Hobbies usually are fertile grounds for flow, but it can also occur in more surprising settings, such as work. For example, I sometimes find myself enjoying a very specific sense of well-being while writing, although that process is very challenging for me compared to other personal or professional activities.

The other major finding of interest concerning flow for our purposes is that researchers have learned it is possible to create the experience, or at least to facilitate its occurrence. In other words, people can do something about adding flow, and the benefits that come with it, to their lives. Consequently, it might be useful for readers to take a moment to identify personal as well as interpersonal areas of life that provide this type of experience. They can also be listed in journal form, of course. Thinking about where one "flows" in life may be more valuable than meets the eye, because knowing where to find it and then spending more time there can add to one's sense of well-being in two ways: while doing the activity and by increasing positive experiences in general.

Increasing and Benefiting from Positive Emotions

On one hand, Fredrickson's work on positive emotions showed that they undo some of the destructive impact created by negative emotions and experiences. On the other, the same research indicated that positive emotions also broaden our perception and stimulate us to consider exploring new possibilities in life. In a very real sense, then, positive experiences, such as flow, offer a unique type of two-for-one bargain in life, not to mention the possibility of helping to start an upward cycle. Although researchers have difficulty determining how many good experiences it takes to offset a bad one, or how often one has to have positive experiences to start an upward cycle, few dispute their importance for well-being.

For example, an obvious way positive emotions influence well-being is that they can reduce stress. Another is that having more positive experiences is associated with at least one type of well-being, namely, the pleasant, fun, or hedonic type. Building on these findings, therapists have applied this information to their work with clients through what is known as *positive therapy* (Seligman, Steen, Park, & Peterson, 2005). One of the most well-researched and best supported positive practices, for instance, involves identifying three good things (or *blessings*, as other researchers call them in similar work) that happen in a day and then taking the time to write about why they are good. Doing this simple activity only once a day, every day, for a week was found to increase measurements of well-being up to a month later. Continuing the exercise for a month produces effects that last much longer, up to six months by some measures.

For this activity to be successful enough to increase well-being in a measurable way, three rules must be followed. First, just counting one's good things or blessings at the end of the day is not enough—one must write them down. Second, it is also necessary to write out a description of why the good things or blessings are good. Again, the act of writing seems to create more deep learning than just noticing something and, therefore, has a better chance of altering cognitive and perhaps even neural patterns. Finally, these good things or blessings need not be major, life-altering ones for the desired effect to occur. Just as we saw with enhancing self-esteem in the last chapter, smaller events are actually more important because they occur more frequently. In other words, processing positive information more often helps shift perception in general so that it is more attuned to the world in more realistically positive ways.

Another activity involving positive feelings, emotions, and behaviors that seems to increase well-being is based on what is called *acts of kindness*. One version of this idea involves doing five random (spontaneous) acts of kindness one day a week for several weeks. Experiments done using pre- and postassessment based on this technique and variations of it show that it works to increase one's sense of well-being (Lyubomirsky, 2001). In addition, this research also points out that the size of the act does not matter as much as being attuned to possibilities in this way. In fact, people are advised to avoid larger acts of kindness as they seem to detract from the value of the activity.

Although the positive effects of the kindness activity do not last as long for the individual as the other positive practice does, expressing kindness has broader social potential. For example, I know of one university where the student psychology club helps sponsor a "kindness day" on campus during which students, staff, and faulty encourage everyone to do small but random acts of kindness in a community-based fashion. And, of course, a much larger version of this type of activity has been going on for years in what is known as Random Acts of Kindness Day (2017) in various countries around the world, including the United States.

The connection between positive psychology and self-esteem for either activity, of course, is grounded in spending time on contemplating or doing worthy things in life more often. Accordingly, the thought activity presented in Box 5.1a may be helpful to those who want to think about these activities in a more active fashion. M's completed form is presented first to illustrate its use, which is followed by a blank form in Box 5.1b. Note that as with the cognitive reframing and problem-solving activities, this one is based on existing research that is well-accepted in the field. Of course, the practice is modified for use with the two-factor approach to enhancing authentic self-esteem and increasing well-being.

In addition to raising awareness concerning the presence of positive self-esteem moments and potential sources of self-esteem that occur in everyday life,

Box 5.1a

Thought Activity: Making Positive Self-Esteem Moments Count

1a. Note a self-esteem moment you experienced and identify which components were present.
Example: Someone thanked me today for using my ability with numbers to help her solve an accounting problem at work. That made me feel good, at least for a time.

1b. Describe which source(s) of self-esteem the experience reflects and why it is good.
Example: Well, that might not seem like such a big deal because it was just work, and we all have skin in the game, as they say. But now that I think about it, there is a self-esteem moment here I usually ignore. After all, the ability to handle numbers well compared to others has been part of my identity ever since I was a little girl. Being competent in this way at work affirms my sense of self because it means that I make a difference at work!

2a. Note a self-esteem moment you experienced and identify which components were present.
Example: I had a terrible day today, and nothing seemed to go well. But when I came home, my child ran to the door and gave me a big hug. Then she said, "Mommy I have been waiting all day to see you. I am glad you are here."

2b. Describe which source(s) of self-esteem the experience reflects and why it is good.
Example: Well, that experience certainly feels good. It surely makes the day seem better. Seeing that look of admiration and joy in my child's eyes makes me feel accepted and valued in a special way. I guess I am worth more than I thought!

3a. Note a self-esteem moment you experienced and identify which components were present.
Example: I stood up for someone even though it was unpopular to take that position.

3b. Describe which source(s) of self-esteem the experience reflects and why it is good.
Example: Even though I was nervous, I stood up for what was just and right, kind of like John Milton talked about. Doing good things like that involves both knowing what is worthwhile or right and standing up for it publically like I did today took some courage to pull off. I guess this combination of worthiness and competence is what people call virtue and it surely is good for my self-esteem!

Box 5.1b

THOUGHT ACTIVITY: MAKING POSITIVE SELF-ESTEEM MOMENTS COUNT

1a. Note a self-esteem moment you experienced and identify which
    components were present.

_____

_____

_____

1b. Describe which source(s) of self-esteem the experience reflects and why it
    is good.

_____

_____

_____

2a. Note a self-esteem moment you experienced and identify which
    components were present.

_____

_____

_____

2b. Describe which source(s) of self-esteem the experience reflects and why it
    is good.

_____

_____

_____

3a. Note a self-esteem moment you experienced and identify which
    components were present.

_____

_____

_____

3b. Describe which source(s) of self-esteem the experience reflects and why it is good.

_____

_____

_____

_____

part of the rationale behind this practice rests on the research concerning positive emotions and the way the brain is designed to recognize patterns. In other words, to some extent, recalling or reviewing experiences often rekindles some of the emotions they involved, as anyone who has reminisced about pleasant times with another person can testify. The process might be analogous to the act of watching a favorite movie again, listening to a meaningful song once more, or returning to an inspiring book.

In other words, focusing on positive self-esteem moments is much better than ruminating on negative ones because reliving emotional events seems to be a way of reexperiencing life that is conducive to the self-enhancement function of self-esteem. Reviewing these experiences, identifying their particular sources of self-esteem, and reflecting on why they are good on a regular basis may also weaken old or negative mental and emotional patterns. Perhaps regular practice could even help stimulate an upward cycle of positive emotion conducive to self-esteem and well-being. These factors and possibilities are among the reasons my work on self-esteem seldom focuses on negative events and experiences.

SELF-ESTEEM, PURPOSE, AND WELL-BEING

Earlier I wrote that although happiness and satisfaction are related, they also differ in that while happiness is based more on feelings and emotions, satisfaction is strongly tied to meaning. It was also suggested that one type of meaning appears to be especially important for mental health, namely, that which comes from having a sense of purpose in life. Having one usually involves trying to live up to that which one values most. This phenomenon means, among other things, that values are important for well-being. Caring for a family, being dedicated to a type of work, and connecting to a larger sense of community are examples of how values and goals work together to create a sense of purpose that makes life satisfyingly meaningful despite its hardships—sometimes, perhaps, even because of them.

Purpose is important for well-being because it unifies behavior and integrates it by providing a sense of personal and social direction. In fact, the relationship between self-esteem, purpose, and well-being lies at the heart of the terror management theory covered in chapter 2. Remember, this view of self-esteem portrays life as something that is, essentially, "nasty, brutish, and short" (Hobbes, 1651/1994) and advances the existential idea that the only way people can live with this terrifying fact is to develop a sense of purpose. Doing something meaningful with the time one does have is helpful because a deep sense of purpose allows us to psychologically transcend the awful awareness that in the not too distant future, we will die.

There are alternatives to finding meaning that bring temporary relief from this terrible fact, of course. At best, they focus only on the immediate gratification of basic needs, pursuing pleasure for as long as one can, or simply giving up, all of which would only hasten an already ugly enough fate. To lessen the existential terror known as death and to prevent such negative and destructive behavior, each society provides pathways to living a meaningful life that makes the burden of being human worthwhile. The sense of meaning necessary to create purpose in this way is most easily seen in belief systems that are bigger than the self.

Consequently, religion, philosophy, and some forms of community, such as those found in family or in making a commitment to a social cause, help people cope with their condition in these and other ways. Living up to the larger beliefs and the values associated with these meaning systems simultaneously protect individuals from harsh realities, offer them a path toward a reasonable degree of well-being, and help create the type of social integration conducive to mental health and well-being that Ryff and Singer (1998) talked about. In this sense, positive and negative self-esteem moments do function as a type of internal compass, just as terror management theory might claim.

Purpose and Intrinsic Values

However, it would be a mistake to think that purposefulness is a mechanistic process that simply requires blind obedience to a system of values and rules. Indeed, today there is so much freedom to choose in life that often people must actively seek out their own pathways of meaning. Consequently, the key to the process seems to involve finding positive values that are intrinsically appealing enough to a given individual that he or she chooses to autonomously pursue them.

Intrinsic values are those positive interests and characteristics that emerge from each individual's particular combination of temperament, personality, and inclinations that serve to make each person a unique human being. Examples of the pursuit of these values are easier to see in children because no external motivation is necessary to generate their willingness to engage in the activities that reflect what they seek out in this way. Instead, they spontaneously appreciate, work at, and enjoy those activities because they are natural to them. Where one child is captivated in this way by sports, for instance, another finds math to be intrinsically interesting. Where a third person pursues music because of its intrinsic value, a fourth finds helping others to be satisfying in this way.

As will be shortly shown, many of the intrinsic values that make people unique also reflect deeper ones that positive psychologists call *virtues* (Coopersmith, 1967; Peterson & Seligman, 2004), something that considerably expands the self-esteem picture in terms of the importance of the worthiness factor. In a word, these values and the virtues they reflect are conducive to well-being because they bring a deeper sense of personal satisfaction to an individual who gives them time. Consequently, certain intrinsic values are among those that give life meaning and purpose, which is one reason it is important to *know oneself* as humanistic psychologists are fond of saying.

Again, Kernis (2003) has done considerable work in this dimension of self-esteem. One of his most important findings in this area concerns a clear relationship between intrinsic values, autonomy, and self-esteem. For example, it turns out that knowing what is worthwhile to oneself as a person, having enough self-esteem to risk affirming it when challenges or opportunities arise, and then coming up with the courage to act autonomously in these ways all work together to create the sense of direction and meaning in life that most call a sense of purpose or purposefulness. Since purpose is related to mental health in Ryff and Singer's (1998) model, it stands to reason that the more people know about the values and characteristics that are most satisfying in this way, the more they might be able to make them a part of their lives and thereby increase well-being.

Social scientists, guidance counselors, and mental health professionals often use values clarification tests to help people develop a clearer sense of what their deeper, more sustaining interests might be. Although complete objectivity is probably not possible for any test that asks people to evaluate themselves, it is helpful to be able to compare our values to those of others and then use that information to develop a sense of which directions to pursue in life. Some vocational tests, such as the Strong Vocational Interest Inventory (Donnay, Morris, Schaubhut, & Thompson, 2004), for example, are particularly good at helping people identify occupational values and that information is useful for selecting career paths. In fact, I have successfully used that instrument in clinical practice as well as for myself when making my own career decisions.

Although such tests tell nothing about one's ability to be successful in this or that line of work, they do identify basic intrinsic interests that appeal to people who select and stay in a given occupation or line of work. Such information is usually helpful in making career choices that have a good chance of satisfying an individual's intrinsic values. Such work helps well-being because of what is called a good *person–environment fit*. This type of situation offers many opportunities to maximize one's potentials and thereby achieve a meaningful degree of well-being.

The benefit of doing work that is satisfying in this way is that it is likely to make life seem more purposeful and worthwhile despite challenges that will arise. For instance, as a boy I sometimes helped my father earn money for the family, as many children have done throughout time and history. As we did our respective jobs together, he made this very observation in a way that always stuck with me. "Son," he said, "when you are grown up, you will find yourself spending most of your time working. If you are smart, you will pick something you like doing." For once, I followed his advice and found that he was right and still is today.

Sometimes wisely choosing in this way is a matter of luck, but it does not have to be that way. The psychological reason behind my father's sage advice is, in part, an important connection between intrinsic values, one's autonomy, authentic self-esteem, and a deeper, more satisfying sense of well-being. In contrast to the more pleasurable hedonic form of happiness discussed earlier, *eudaimonic* well-being, as positive psychologists often call it, has to do with living the good life. Aristotle described this way of living and the values associated with it in terms of maximizing one's potential as a unique individual as much as possible.

The connection between living this type of good life, authentic self-esteem, and well-being can be described in the following way. Intrinsic human values and interests, such as love of learning about something, being creative in a given area, caring for others in ways that improve their lives, and so on, are seen as being inherently worthy or good. Exercising one's autonomy as a person allows him or her to pursue these good things whenever possible. Pursuing good things in this way creates a sense of purpose. Living with a sense of purpose requires facing challenges in ways that demonstrate competence and worthiness. Such authentic actions positively affect self-esteem and increase well-being.

The Connection between Intrinsic Values and Virtue

Aristotle developed one of the first criteria to evaluate whether a particular human characteristic is virtuous. According to his classificatory system, many human characteristics may be lived in terms of *excess* (too much of some trait), *defect* (too little of some trait), or a balance between those two states, which Aristotle called the *intermediate* or *golden mean*. Most important to our purposes is one virtue in particular that he expressed in the following way: "With regard to honour and dishonour the mean is proper pride, the excess is known as a sort of 'empty vanity,' and the deficiency is undue humility" (McKeon, 1941, p. 960). In a real sense, the modern-day language for the psychological space Aristotle called *proper pride* may be nothing other than what we call *authentic self-esteem*. For instance, we saw in chapter 1 that an excess of worthiness, which is a sense of worthiness that is not earned and thereby balanced by competence, results in problems associated with the most extreme forms of vanity, such as narcissism. And the type of humility that results from a lack of competence, such as being unable to stand up for oneself when necessary, would also be likely to be unhealthy because of an excess in the other direction.

More recently, positive psychology has developed an assessment instrument that is based on a certain type of values called *virtues*. One such project, called VIA for Values in Action (Peterson & Seligman, 2004), is an international effort and its values test has been taken by hundreds of thousands of people around the world. This particular instrument is only concerned with values that are seen as intrinsically worthy by their very nature, which is why they may be seen as virtuous.

The developers of the instrument began by identifying the particular characteristics people seem to value about human beings as found in many religions, philosophies, and cultures around the world, both present and past. Then, these traits were subjected to an evaluation process based on several criteria. One of them, for example, is whether a quality is something that people widely appreciate when it is present in an individual and disapprove of when it is not, such as the difference between courage and cowardice. If a particular characteristic passes these tests, then it is identified as a valued human characteristic that is inherently worthwhile for a person to possess or to pursue. In a word, it is *worthy* in the sense that I have been using the term.

This work resulted in the identification of 24 highly valued personal characteristics. Many of them share central features so they can be grouped together on that basis. The unifying theme connecting several such characteristics is called a basic *human virtue*, of which there are six (Peterson & Seligman, 2004, pp. 29–30). Some of them are clearly connected to what we know about authentic self-esteem. For example, the virtue of temperance (moderation) involves self-control, and courage (authenticity) is often necessary to make virtuous self-esteem choices when challenged to do the right thing under trying circumstances. In the next chapter, we will see that traits reflecting the virtue of humanity (care for others) include several interpersonal behaviors related to healthy self-esteem as it occurs in relationships.

The VIA test instrument is designed to identify 24 valued human characteristics, the behavioral traits that reflect them in everyday life, and the underlying virtues they reflect. The results of the assessment even include the relative strength of each such possibility for any given individual by presenting the characteristics one seems to value the most in descending order of importance. The top five are considered to be especially important because they are strong enough to manifest in an individual's general behavior. Since these underlying values and the character traits associated with them are intrinsic to a given individual in this way, they are seen as signature strengths.

According to this view, expressing such strengths not only affirms the underlying positive values they represent but also usually results in very satisfying activity because it is intrinsic to one's make-up as a person. Affirming such core interests also makes a connection to deeper human values because they reflect broader and more basic virtues. Consequently, the process of living a more virtuous or good life in this way generates the type of satisfaction that comes from a richer sense of well-being than can be reached hedonically. In other words, knowing about these interests and understanding their value can lead to something of a win–win for an individual, those around him or her, and well-being. In fact, positive psychologists developed an activity based on exercising one's signature strengths to help people increase such virtuous behavior in everyday life. Testing people before and after engaging in such an activity on a regular basis leads to a measurably greater sense of well-being (Duckworth, Steen, & Seligman, 2005).

INCREASING SELF-ESTEEM, VIRTUE, AND WELL-BEING

As much as this line of reasoning makes good sense, an open discussion of something like virtue and researching it scientifically is a relatively new development in social science. At least in my opinion, all too often social science tends to avoid identifying one set of values as being more desirable than others. Instead, many social scientists advocate the position that values are simply culturally relative. However, within the context of the two-factor definition of self-esteem, certain values found in some cultures, such as the horrible racism found in Nazi culture, are neither valuable nor valid because authentic self-esteem cannot be based on doing bad things well. Thus, we have a problem that needs to be resolved before going any further.

Religious leaders and philosophers are free to discuss values and virtues based on beliefs or arguments. However, studying values or virtues scientifically requires more evidence, especially if one is interested in determining whether some values are better than others for people in general. Another problem is that social science generally attributes such things as values and virtues to environment and culture. Of course, there is much truth to this position because we know how widely values vary from culture to culture and from people to people, especially across time and throughout history.

However, some social scientists, such as those who advocate more radical schools of what is called *constructionism* (Raskin, 2002) go so far as to maintain that all realities are socially constructed, which would mean that there is no such thing as true values or real virtues, including those that are good or right as Milton intended. Others are often afraid to discuss values simply because they fear being seen as politically incorrect or culturally insensitive.

Fortunately, support is now growing for the idea that certain values, including some of those described as virtues, really are more valuable because they are important to most people and may even help the species survive. In addition to the work done on values by positive psychologists in the VIA project as well as in the field of self-esteem (Mruk & Skelly, 2017), for example, evolutionary psychologists note striking similarities between the behavior of certain primates and human beings. These findings suggest that some preferences are hardwired into our brains as a form of biological or inherent value among primates. One, for instance, comes from work with certain monkeys showing that they mirror behavior much as children do. It is now known that such imitative behavior involves neurological structures found in both types of brains called *mirror neurons*. They seem to play an important role in acquiring the social behaviors that are valuable to animals that depend on working together as a group to survive.

Some comparative and evolutionary researchers suggest that something similar might occur with empathy, another ability that is helpful for social creatures that depend on one another. For example, like human infants, under certain conditions some animals will make comforting gestures toward another one when it shows obvious signs of distress. Other work in this area notes that a few primates also exhibit what might be called *basic social behavior*. Some monkeys, for instance, form complex social hierarchies in which they come to have a particular place or role and others seem to form lasting social relationships that are important for their well-being—just like humans or, perhaps, the other way around.

Finally, although a bit more speculative, there are stirrings of work indicating that some of the more evolved species of primates may develop a very rudimentary sense of the value of fair treatment or justice, something that is helpful in facilitating basic prosocial behavior (Bekoff & Pierce, 2009). In this case, two monkeys learn to do a task next to each other and then receive a bit of food as reinforcement. At one point, the experimenter will give one monkey a treat instead of ordinary food but not the other. The one who is treated less favorably, in turn, may actually refuse to do the task again for regular monkey food. It is as though this monkey says something like, "Hey, this is unfair. We are doing the same work here, and the other guy gets more. That is an injustice, and I protest!"

In short, there are grounds to accept the arguments used by humanistic and positive psychologists that affirm the existence of more basic or human values. These *universal values*, if we may call them that, may be seen as virtuous because they provide foundations for a good or, at least, satisfying life. The emerging evidence of the biological foundations for some of these basic qualities offers some support for this position. At the very least, it seems reasonable to conclude that it is not possible to support a completely relativistic position concerning the links between basic values, virtue, and well-being.

In practice, there are at least two ways to use information on virtues and values to enhance authentic self-esteem and general well-being. The first is to explore these values more fully by taking the VIA test or something like it and using it as previously discussed. Since virtue is a source of self-esteem and since the VIA program is based on virtue, using that approach should have a positive effect on both self-esteem and well-being. The test has been free and available to the public through the Internet and can be accessed with any standard search engine. In fact, I have suggested using these types of instruments as a part of classes I teach on well-being, when working with clients, and for myself.

The results are consistently impressive. For instance, although some of mine change from time to time, the characteristic called a *love of learning*, which is a reflection of the deeper value concerning *wisdom/knowledge*, shows up first on my list time and time again. Accordingly, it is not surprising that I chose academic work and will continue to do that past normal retirement age. The other four top values also stand as character strengths because they are rooted in one's personality according to this instrument, but I have found they move about a bit in a way that reflects shifting priorities as life changes. Even so, one or two of them always remain. Consequently, I only concentrate on a few of the values and valued traits in my work—perhaps two, and three at most. Of course, other lists are available too, such as those contained within various religious or philosophical systems. Their value has been supported for centuries, although not empirically.

Another way to find out about these *double values* (intrinsic and virtuous), if I may call them that, may be to rely on one's own ability to examine his or her life and then identify times in it that seem to be most satisfying or meaningful personally and interpersonally. Those that occurred in positive self-esteem moments are especially desirable for anyone interested in the connection between authentic self-esteem, virtue, and well-being. Exercising those particular values may be a clearer, or at least more theoretically consistent, pathway to strengthening the relationship between authentic self-esteem and well-being than does using a more general approach.

A thought activity is illustrated in Box 5.2a as a guide for those who do not wish to take a test but who still want to find out something about their

---

Box 5.2a

THOUGHT ACTIVITY: IDENTIFYING INTRINSIC VALUES
AS WELL-BEING STRENGTHS

1a. I feel that I am most meaningfully engaged or satisfied with life when I? (*Describe* activity.)
Am fully involved in trying to find a new way of doing something in an area I am interested in, especially if I have to do some research to get there.

1b. This activity reflects the value of _____? (*Identify* a positive value related to well-being.)
You know, I spend a lot of time learning about things in this particular area and although it is hard work, I enjoy the challenge very much. That probably means I value learning a lot.

1c. This value is one of my strengths because _____. (*Write* a reason supporting this observation, such as why the quality is valuable.)
Valuing learning is a strength because it helps deal with problems. Plus, it has practical value such as increasing my competence, which improves my chances of getting a promotion.

2a. I feel that I am most meaningfully engaged or satisfied with life when I? (*Describe* activity.)
Go to church, meditate, or visit a museum. I know that sounds kind of traditional, but I like the feeling of connection with something bigger than myself I get there.

2b. This activity reflects the value of _____? (*Identify* a positive value related to well-being.)
Well, there is some form of "spiritual" value here. I don't know if it is religious or psychological, but I feel more hopeful during these times and for a while afterward too.

2c. This value is one of my strengths because _____. (*Write* a reason supporting this observation, such as why the quality is valuable.)
Knowing how to find hope is a strength because it gives me a different perspective on things when life is tough. It is a way of stepping outside of myself and finding inspiration or peace that I can usually count on.

3a. I feel that I am most meaningfully engaged or satisfied with life when I? (*Describe* activity.)
Am able to get other people to open up, relax, enjoy themselves, feel accepted, and laugh.

3b. This activity reflects the value of _____? (*Identify* a positive value related to well-being.)
Well, I guess taking the time to help others see the brighter side of life by laughing probably means that I value humor.

3c. This value is one of my strengths because _____. (*Write* a reason supporting this observation, such as why the quality is valuable.)
Having a good sense of humor may not seem like much of a strength at first. But it does help me out when I'm stressed because it reminds me that a given problem is usually not the end of the world. Other people also seem to seek me out more often because we often laugh together. So I guess humor has some social as well as personal worth.

---

own intrinsic values and think about how to use them more effectively in ways that could make life more meaningful. As usual, a blank version follows in Box 5.2b for those who wish to try the activity and/or make it a part of a self-esteem journal. Note that it is also possible to revisit one's responses from time to time to track or revise one's values, virtues, and their related possibilities.

Remembering the material on increasing self-esteem in chapter 4, it is also fairly easy to develop self-esteem action plans designed to increase the frequency of these virtuous forms of competence and worthiness. For instance, in M's case corresponding ways to increase the use of positive traits to enhance well-being might include working toward obtaining a credential, such as a certificate or degree, indicating competence in a given area of intrinsic value. Alternatively, she could work on increasing a sense of worthiness in her life by doing volunteer work that uses her ability to help others who cannot help themselves. Setting up such a well-being goal is consistent with both the psychology of self-esteem based on a two-factor approach and with the principles of positive psychology being explored in this chapter. Consequently, it is reasonable to think that a virtuous self-esteem action plan would create a synergistic effect on self-esteem and mental health.

Box 5.2b

1a. I feel that I am most meaningfully engaged or satisfied with life when I? (*Describe* activity).

_____

1b. This activity reflects the value of _____? (*Identify* a positive value related to well-being.)

_____

1c. This value is one of my strengths because _____. (*Write* a reason supporting this observation, such as why the quality is valuable.)

_____

2a. I feel that I am most meaningfully engaged or satisfied with life when I? (*Describe* activity.)

_____

2b. This activity reflects the value of _____? (*Identify* a positive value related to well-being.)

_____

2c. This value is one of my strengths because _____. (*Write* a reason supporting this observation, such as why the quality is valuable.)

_____

3a. I feel that I am most meaningfully engaged or satisfied with life when I? (*Describe* activity.)

_____

3b. This activity reflects the value of _____? (*Identify* a positive value related to well-being.)

_____

3c. This value is one of my strengths because _____. (*Write* a reason supporting this observation, such as why the quality is valuable.)

_____

As an aside, I often wonder which of these basic, intrinsic, virtuous, good, worthy or double values appeal to any given reader. The reason for my curiosity is that I suspect if he or she started to express one or two of them in daily life more often, he or she might help trigger a positive self-fulfilling cycle of satisfaction and meaning or purpose. To put it another way, a well-supported secret to well-being is to start doing less of what one knows one should not do and begin doing more of what one knows as interesting, meaningful, and virtuous! The details will often take care of themselves.

6

Beyond the Self

Authentic Self-Esteem, Relationships, and More

The last dimension of self-esteem to consider in this book concerns a link between authentic self-esteem, well-being, and the larger human community. Being a part of the human community includes relationships, of course, but more. As mentioned in the last chapter, Ryff and Singer (1998) talked about this dimension of mental health in terms of social integration and social cohesion.

It is possible to illustrate the link between relationships and well-being by using what is called the *deathbed test*. Aristotle may have been the first to develop this test as a way of helping people understand what is important in life (Kristjansson, 2013). However, Christopher Peterson and Martin Seligman (2004) offer a version of it that positive psychologists use to do similar work. The test involves asking a person to imagine himself or herself at the end of life and being presented with a question. It reads something like, "What do you think you would wish that you had done more of in your life when you had the chance?" People seldom reply with answers like "made more money," "had more fun," or other hedonic possibilities. Instead, they typically wish they had spent more time with others who are important to them, especially loved ones. Indeed, one person close to me said that very thing just before he died. The point is that this quick existential exercise can be quite powerful, especially if it reminds people to pay more attention to their loved ones and the value of the time spent with them.

So strong is the connection between interpersonal relationships, mental health, and well-being that many social scientists consider relationships to be a *deep structure* (Myers, 2000). Deep structures are thought to be necessary for basic as well as healthy human functioning. For example, one deep structure we all have some experience with is language. People who study language, especially psycholinguistic theorists, focus on the fact that the human brain comes hardwired for language, something like how a computer comes equipped to accept programs. However, also like a computer, language does not occur unless the software necessary to activate this brain-based function is installed. Such programming only comes through relationships with caregivers who communicate and interact with us as the brain develops. In other words, although nature provides the possibility of language, it is relationships that allow us to have a meaningful connection with the larger human community.

For instance, most people are likely to have read or heard about feral children or children who were severely neglected and locked away in closets at an early age without the ability to interact verbally with others. Although the rehabilitation of their linguistic capacity is possible, it is also a very difficult process, the outcome of which depends on age and degree of neglect. On a more positive note, the wonderful capacity of this deep structure to make life meaningful can be seen in people who are born deaf and learn sign language to fully express themselves. But learning sign language, it should be noted, also involves interacting with others. Even exceptional figures, such as Helen Keller, needed the touch of another person to be able to communicate. The particular sensory path used to communicate does not seem to matter: Having and activating the deep structure with and through relationships does.

Relationships also seem to stand as a deep structure for authentic self-esteem and well-being. Many may think that since self-esteem focuses on the self, that work in this area is only concerned with the individual, and, to be sure, most of it is. However, the field also studies the ways in which self-esteem plays a role in the social dimensions of life. How relationships are connected to worthiness, how the functions of self-esteem help regulate relationships in positive or in negative ways, and how self-esteem works in regard to developing a larger sense of community are three important themes in the social psychology of self-esteem. Since all of these processes are related to happiness, satisfaction with life, and well-being, it is necessary to examine what we now know about self-esteem in relationships. This information may even lead to some suggestions concerning how to go about increasing authentic self-esteem in the context of a relationship, something I call *relational* self-esteem, and well-being in general.

SELF-ESTEEM IN RELATIONSHIPS: MUTUAL SELF-REGULATION

A good portion of the work on self-esteem and relationships concerns the two factors that create authentic self-esteem and their respective sources. For example, worthiness is strongly connected to our relationships, and interacting with others is instrumental in providing the basic sense of acceptance that is necessary for the formation of identity as well as self-esteem. A large part of how we come to know ourselves, including our worth or value as a person, is through the reactions others have to us in our interactions with them. We learn things about ourselves, both pleasant and otherwise, through the eyes of another, so to speak. The great sociologist George Herbert Mead (1934) described the portion of one's identity that comes from interactions with others as the *looking glass self*, which means we come to know ourselves by seeing ourselves through the eyes of another, actually many others.

For self-esteem, the love of a parent, the kindness of an aunt, the interest of a teacher, the support of a friend, the advice of a mentor, the acceptance of a group, and many other social interactions are all ways of being connected to others that have an impact on the worthiness factor. Sometimes, of course, others reflect back the opposite type of message, which results in feeling insecure about one's merit or value as a person. Even if that occurs in childhood when acceptance is so important, good enough acceptance can be found later through other connections to humanity, such as friendship, group membership, a sense of religious community, and, of course, with a therapist. The connection between interpersonal phenomena, and mutual self-regulation also occurs in the other two domains of self-esteem associated with its worthiness factor. For example, how others react to our physical appearance, and we to theirs, involves reciprocal interaction. Similarly, virtue or morality often occurs in an interpersonal context.

While it is true that the worthiness component of self-esteem is most active in the interpersonal domains of life that pertain to self-esteem, the two-factor model maintains that authentic self-esteem is based on a relationship between competence and worthiness. Consequently, it should not be difficult to point out how competence plays a real, although perhaps a lesser, role in determining relational happiness and well-being. Research along this line shows that competence helps one achieve relationship satisfaction in several ways. Social competencies, for instance, are necessary to initiate a relationship or to respond to invitations about having one. Interpersonal abilities are required for one to be emotionally supportive in ways that nurture or enhance a relationship. Having the capacity to effectively manage interpersonal conflicts that occur in relationships is necessary to sustain them over time. Finally, of course, all of these interpersonal skills depend on one's ability to communicate effectively, which points to yet another set of relational competencies to acquire for relationships to function well (Buhrmester, Furman, Wittenberg, & Reis, 1988).

It is necessary to appreciate one more general feature about the way self-esteem and social factors work together before dealing with particulars. It is that social interaction is a two-way street and may even be a multiple-way street if more than two people are involved, something akin to how a traffic circle works on roads. It is important to note this point because classical theories of causality portray the world in terms of causes and effects. This lineal approach is often likened to a billiard ball view of causality because every time the cue ball strikes another on the table, a clear equal and opposite reaction occurs. In this sense, the cue ball is the cause or independent variable and the corresponding change in state and direction of the other is the effect or dependent variable.

Some scientists, including social scientists, favor such models of causality because, in part, they appear to make connecting events fairly straightforward. However, others have moved beyond such simplistic thinking and toward understanding causality as a more circular or reciprocal process. This view takes into account the fact that various components in a relationship affect each other in an interactive or back-and-forth fashion. Such a dynamic view of causality is much more useful for describing complex phenomena, and there may be nothing more complex than human behavior. Consequently, when I say there is a relationship between self-esteem and something else—in this case, relationships—it means that the variables affect each other to create an outcome, not that one variable determines the other.

In other words, it makes no sense to talk about either the chicken (self-esteem) or the egg (relationships). Instead, it is important to appreciate how one shapes the other. This type of dynamic was seen, for example, in the connection between self-esteem, relational (marital) happiness, and well-being identified earlier. What this type of causality means for self-esteem in relationships is that while the actions and reactions others express toward an individual may have a positive or negative impact on that person's self-esteem, his or her self-esteem also influences the ways in which people act and react to him or her in the first place! There are many other examples of this type of relational reciprocity in life, such as in whether poor parenting leads to a difficult child or if a difficult child makes for poor parenting. The fact of the matter is that very little in relationships is simple because their variables interact with each other and do so over time, which makes the process an ever-changing dynamic.

Authentic Self-Esteem as a Relational Variable

Fortunately, work concerning self-esteem and relationships goes well beyond these general findings concerning worth, acceptance, competence, and reciprocity, as important as they are. Today we know more specific information about how high and low self-esteem affect relationships, and vice versa. In fact, I developed a list of several major findings researchers in this area have uncovered over the years (Mruk, 2013b). Some of them may help us understand how self-esteem and relationships work together to foster the development of personal and interpersonal well-being. For example, this work shows that people with high self-esteem usually focus on their partner's positive personal characteristics more than their negative ones. Such *positive illusions*, as they are sometimes called, are likely to make the relationship more enjoyable for both people. The effect may even strengthen if both partners have a higher degree of self-esteem, since that additional factor increases the possibility of upward relational cycles (Sciangula & Morry, 2009).

One can access this finding experientially by simply remembering how wonderful a loved one seemed to be earlier in the relationship. It is often as though the person was perfect in so many ways. Of course, individuals still have their flaws but focusing on the good points minimizes such blemishes and makes positive interactions more likely, especially if the other reciprocates. The so-called honeymoon phase of a relationship also involves this phenomenon, and it helps sustain relationships as they become more realistic. Such mutual acceptance feels good for both parties and can boost their sense of worth strongly enough to positively affect self-esteem. By contrast, people with low or defensive self-esteem are found to be more likely to focus on the negative characteristics of themselves or the other, which decreases the frequency of positive interactions and reduces happiness, satisfaction, and well-being, often for both.

Similarly, this line of work indicates that playfulness is more frequent in relationships where both individuals have higher levels of self-esteem (Aune & Wong, 2002). In this case, self-esteem is thought to be related to the ability to let go of worries about rejection and take appropriate risks more freely, something that often increases spontaneity in the relationship. If reciprocated, the result of this self-esteem-based relational dynamic is often a creative, moment-to-moment way of connecting with the other that is likely to generate interpersonal forms of flow. Having fun with someone recreationally or being immersed in conversation with another for an extended period can be examples of such flow states if the interaction is challenging enough, but there are many more interpersonal possibilities too. In other words, playfulness has the capacity to broaden perspectives and build possibilities within a relational context. It is easy to see, for instance, that families and couples with high self-esteem seem to enjoy each other and enjoy spending time with each other.

Although seldom talked about, self-esteem seems to play a role in generating intimate sexual relationships (Menard & Offman, 2009). The degree of vulnerability necessary to reach a deep level of acceptance in this area of life requires trust, another positive emotion, as well as playful spontaneity. This process is also reciprocal: Being open or trusting requires some degree of acceptance by the other and being accepted by the other simultaneously makes being open or trusting more possible. The result is a mutually given series of affirmations that can spiral to a meaningful as well as satisfying conclusion about one's worth as a person. To make things even more interesting, the same work indicates that self-esteem is involved with men's and women's sexuality in somewhat different ways. Performance appears to be more important to men with low self-esteem than to those with higher levels. Women with high self-esteem tend to be more selective in regard to identifying and accepting sexual partners than are men in general, and these women also tend to be more selective than those with lower self-esteem (Zeigler-Hill, Campe, & Myers, 2009).

More research indicates that self-esteem is connected to relationships in another important positive fashion: Self-esteem plays a role in determining whether relationships last over time. One finding supporting this position is that people with high self-esteem have been found to be less vulnerable to things that threaten relationships. For example, the effect that flattery from a third party has on a couple seems to involve self-esteem. People with high self-esteem tend to resist flattery from others more than those with low self-esteem (Gagne, Khan, Lydon, & To, 2008).

This phenomenon is understood to mean that people with high self-esteem are more secure in their sense of being worthy and feel more accepted in their relationships, which creates a greater sense of relational satisfaction and well-being. Thus flattery, perhaps including the flirtatious type, is less meaningful to them. It may even be perceived as an indirect compliment to one's ability to attract a desirable partner. However, those with low self-esteem are more uncertain about their worth or acceptability and are, therefore, more vulnerable to, or interested in, other sources of it. Sometimes this type of accessibility may even constitute a danger to a relationship, especially if it appeals to unmet needs for acceptance and self-esteem.

Another important self-esteem finding related to relational longevity concerns the crucial ability to repair damage in a relationship when things go wrong, such as a mistake, a difficult period, or other problems that may injure or harm a relationship. These situations require the ability to do such things as admit an error, make apologies, accept responsibility, and extend oneself to the other so that the relationship can be nurtured back to health. The processes involved in such behavior usually require temporarily putting one's own needs aside, taking the risk of reaching out to the other in ways that involve being vulnerable to rejection, and then having the ability to competently address the needs of the other first so that the relationship may heal or move forward again. In short, people with high self-esteem see these types of interpersonal behaviors as a priority and tend to engage in such rejection prevention strategies (Berenson & Downey, 2006) more readily. Their sense of worth allows them to be more vulnerable when necessary, and their interpersonal skills are competent enough to generate the helpful behavior.

Problematic Self-Esteem as a Relational Variable

In general, low or defensive self-esteem seems to operate in ways that negatively affect relationships. For example, we saw in chapter 2 that goal setting depends, in part, on self-esteem. Those with high self-esteem tend to use approach-oriented goals when encountering interpersonal problems. This problem-solving style is more effective, it will be recalled, because it involves taking steps necessary to reach a particular point, such as resolving a conflict, rather than wasting psychological resources on other possibilities. By contrast, low or defensive self-esteem tends to result in people being more concerned with protecting themselves against potential dangers, including interpersonal threats. Since avoidance goals also take energy, the individual must spend limited self-regulatory resources on dealing with two problems: the original one in the relationship and the new one generated by taking on the burdensome process of adopting avoidance goals such as rejection or loss. Often the result is an unfortunate concatenation of relational events that only complicates matters.

For instance, one of the most powerful negative impacts that low or defensive self-esteem can have on relationships and well-being involves something called *rejection sensitivity* (Berenson & Downey, 2006). Whether a person admits it or not, rejection is difficult for nearly all human beings. Evidence for this comes from the work discussed while examining self-esteem moments in chapter 3, which showed that two of the most powerful ones involve acceptance and rejection. Being valued by another person in a new or existing relationship can create strong, positive self-esteem moments tied to the worthiness factor of authentic self-esteem. If an individual or group is important in terms of one's identity, then being rejected has an opposite effect. Not only can some types of rejection damage one's sense of worth, but in more extreme cases it can also threaten identity itself. A complete collapse of self-esteem exposes identity to such a high state of threat that it may contribute to such things as suicide and sometimes even homicide. It almost goes without saying that those with extremely low or highly defensive self-esteem are at a proportionally greater risk for such negative possibilities.

Rejection sensitivity is an orientation toward others usually associated with low or defensive self-esteem that involves being overly sensitive, if not hypersensitive, to rejection. This relational stance typically involves paying conscious and unconscious attention to what are called *rejection cues* (indications of possible threats to the relationship). Once they are perceived, an individual may react to them by feeling threatened, which increases the likelihood of engaging in self-protective psychological and interpersonal behavior aimed at avoiding rejection or at least minimizing its impact if it does occur. The particular way in which one expresses rejection sensitivity depends on such things as the characteristics of the relationship, one's personality, cultural mores, and, of course, the type and level of one's self-esteem. However, the cost of being with others in this way is always the same: Maintaining a high degree of vigilance for hints of rejection requires spending considerable psychological resources on avoidance goals and thereby leaves less available for relational enhancement.

Of course, because people differ there are many ways of expressing rejection sensitivity. Some of the relatively subtle or milder of them include being easily hurt by others, avoiding situations in which any form of rejection may occur, or simply distancing oneself from one's partner. Sometimes people who suffer this condition overcompensate for it by looking to others for signs of worth in mildly problematic ways, such as seeking compliments on their appearance, by being "people pleasers" to receive praise and avoid criticism, or through gravitating to partners who are vulnerable themselves and therefore less likely to leave. People with mildly defensive self-esteem often find themselves speaking or acting in ways they later regret as they struggle with protecting their unstable or fragile self-esteem. As seen in chapter 1, low-level self-esteem problems of all types can go on for years, though that does detract from a sense of happiness, satisfaction, and well-being.

Severe degrees of sensitivity to rejection have been found to contribute to more serious relational difficulties, such as chronic criticism of one's partner, unwarranted jealously, constant suspicion, trying to control one's partner, and even health-threatening behaviors, including excessive drinking and lower immune system functioning (DeHart, Tennen, Armeli, Todd, & Afflect, 2008). In fact, it has been found that one's immunological system is affected by the quality of one's marital relationship (Kiecolt-Glaser et al., 1997). Remarkably, immune functioning seems to drop within just a few hours of strongly negative exchanges. To be hyperbolic for a moment, I would rather go to a dentist who does not use

Novocain than have a major argument with my wife because I know the toll will be high regardless of who "wins." In general, it is fair to say that when used excessively, all of these protective maneuvers and their negative interpersonal consequences can evolve into genuine threats to a relationship because rejection sensitivity wears on both partners.

THE SELF-FULFILLING CHARACTER OF SELF-ESTEEM IN RELATIONSHIPS

Earlier in this chapter, I mentioned that the research on self-esteem and relationships indicates they are reciprocally connected, which means that factors affect each other. Similar to previous research on the dynamics of self-esteem discussed earlier concerning positive emotions, researchers who specialize in the area of self-esteem and relationships also characterize the way reciprocity works with them as a self-fulfilling prophecy (Berenson & Downey, 2006). If the goal is to increase authentic self-esteem and well-being in or through relationships, then it is important to know more about the ways in which self-esteem works to help regulate them in this way.

People with low or defensive self-esteem need relationships as much as anyone else and perhaps even more since relationships are a primary source of worth and meaning. Ironically, however, their condition makes the challenges associated with initiating, sustaining, and repairing relationships more difficult. For instance, rejection sensitivity predisposes a person toward being overly vigilant and reactive to perceived threats in a relationship, sometimes even when there aren't any or when the degree of threat is minor and best ignored. Even worse for a relationship, such self-protective behavior as withdrawing or distancing oneself from the other, usually occurs when relational stress is high. Yet, these are the times when relationships need the opposite type of responses, such as opening up, being sensitive, talking about feelings, making amends, expressing affection, and so forth.

Unfortunately, however, if one partner pulls back to protect himself or herself, that reaction can easily threaten someone with low or defensive self-esteem. Such individuals may even perceive withdrawal as proof the partner is thinking about leaving. That perception, in turn, is likely to generate even more self-protective behavior. All too often the result of this type of interpersonal self-esteem dynamic becomes a downward self-fulfilling cycle of negative perceptions, emotions, and behavior. Over time such a negative feedback cycle damages the relationship as well as the individuals in it. In this way, problematic self-esteem quietly helps create the very thing that the individual who suffers it often fears in relationships to begin with, namely, conflict, rejection, and loss (Baldwin, 2006; Berenson & Dowdy, 2006; Leary, 2008; Murray, 2008).

Those with defensive self-esteem are vulnerable to the same self-fulfilling dynamics but tend to live them out in ways that make the situation even more problematic, because unbalanced self-esteem creates more behavioral and relational instability. Consequently, when such individuals perceive threats to a relationship, they tend to defend themselves more aggressively than those with low self-esteem to protect themselves but in very counterproductive ways. For example, self-protective strategies such as excessive criticism (demeaning the other verbally or through gestures), blaming (trying to shift responsibility), stonewalling (refusing to engage the other when legitimate offers to do so are made), and physical, sexual, or emotional abuse take terrible tolls on relationships.

Although certainly not the only cause of it, such negative interpersonal events as abandonment or infidelity may reflect problems with self-esteem in relationships. For instance, a person with low self-esteem might perceive a threat to the relationship and pull away from his or her partner to avoid potential hurt. However, if his or her need for acceptance is great enough, being alone or lonely is also threatening. Thus, finding someone else while still in the relationship could become an attractive self-protective possibility. Likewise, defensive self-esteem might lead to infidelity if sexuality means being successful to a person with competence-based self-esteem issues, because such an interpersonal conquest provides an immediate, albeit distorted, sense of acceptance or worth. Both ways of dealing with relational problems often bring temporary relief to those with problematic self-esteem. However, such tactics usually solve nothing and often put the relationship in jeopardy by stimulating other sets of negative self-fulfilling dynamics that are difficult to heal, such as a betrayal of trust.

If the role of self-esteem in relationships is based on a reciprocal process that has the power to be self-fulfilling in negative ways, then this self-esteem relational dynamic should also be capable of generating positive results as well. In fact, much of the work on self-esteem and relationships focuses on its enhancing function and how healthy self-esteem contributes to satisfying relationships. For example, in addition to perceiving less in the way of unrealistic or minor threats, healthy self-esteem also points people in a more prosocial or positive interpersonal direction. In other words, the motivation that accompanies the expansion function of self-esteem directs one toward reacting and behaving in ways that are genuinely conducive to a mutual, supportive, and growing relationship.

We already saw, for example, how healthy self-esteem is associated with positive relationship dynamics, such as playfulness, openness, sexuality, and, by extension, love as well as care. These and other types of interpersonal behavior also help people to better tolerate the vulnerability and uncertainty that comes from engaging in the nurturing or reparative behaviors necessary to address the needs of a relationship when it is suffering or in danger. Under these conditions self-esteem related behaviors are still reciprocal, but here they work together to create a more positive outcome, even more so if one's partner also possesses a reasonable degree of healthy self-esteem.

As might be expected, the enhancing function of self-esteem helps create a virtuous or upward self-fulfilling cycle instead of the vicious downward one caused by the self-protective function more strongly associated with low or defensive self-esteem. The result of connecting with others based on authentic self-esteem, then, is much more likely to be higher degrees of happiness and satisfaction, because this type of foundation helps create more positive experiences and deeper connections between people. Indeed, some research indicates that one's sense of self, perhaps even measurably so in the area of the brain associated with the self, expands when one is in love, suggesting an increase in, or at least deepening of, being connected with others (Aron, Ketay, Riela, & Aron, 2008). Although more speculative, it is likely that similar patterns may apply to other major forms of relationships, such as friendships and parenting.

It is necessary to appreciate one more thing before examining ways to facilitate more positive or upward relational cycles. Although talking about extremes is helpful for making important points about self-esteem, we saw in chapter 1 that the most common type of self-esteem is medium self-esteem. Thus, it is fair to say that while some relationships may be toxic to self-esteem and that problematic forms of self-esteem can harm relationships, most of us probably have relationships that are more positive than negative. Further, and just as we saw with individual self-esteem and well-being, most people in relationships desire higher levels of satisfaction. This condition is fortunate because it gives us a lot of potential to work with in terms of motivation for healthy relational growth and well-being.

In more concrete terms, it can be said that most people deal with the paradoxical protective and expansion or enhancing functions of self-esteem in their relations. However, since we know that medium self-esteem involves some degree of both competence and worthiness, the majority of us are more motivated by the self-expansion rather than the self-protective function in our relationships. Consequently, while we tend to feel a meaningful degree of satisfaction in our significant connections, we also tend to slip into behaviors associated with the self-protective mode with some regularity. The trick is, of course, to maximize the positive and minimize the negative. Fortunately, recent research offers some things to consider that may be helpful in this regard.

INCREASING RELATIONAL SELF-ESTEEM AND WELL-BEING

Although the next thought activity reflects several things already encountered in this book, it also involves some new information that needs to be appreciated before presenting the concept. John and Julie Gottman (1995) are a couple who research and help long-term relationships, especially troubled ones. In addition to identifying many useful things about the differences between healthy or positive and unhealthy or troubled relationships, they offer two concepts that are relevant here.

One concept is that negative or bad relationship experiences are stronger or more powerful for people than positive or good ones, just as we saw with Fredrickson's work on positive emotions in chapter 2. Similarly, there is reason to believe from her work that positive relational activities can undo negative ones. The point is twofold. First, negative interpersonal behaviors, such as making nasty comments, demeaning the other, failing to care when it is needed, fighting dirty in arguments, holding on to grudges, and various forms of neglect, betrayal, or abuse, are very hard on relationships, the people in them, and, of course, their self-esteem. Second, good relational hygiene involves being mindful of the connection between self-esteem and relationships, especially their reciprocal and self-fulfilling character.

Fredrickson suggested that the magic number of positive experiences necessary to undo a negative one is three. Perhaps reflecting how important relationships are for human beings, John Gottman (1995) reportedly suggested that, in general, at least five positive relational interactions are necessary to offset a single negative one. Both numbers are flawed because such things as the intensity, significance, and duration of experiences vary. In fact, Fredrickson has already revised her calculation. However, as a social scientist, I like to see two independent lines of work come to similar conclusions because this type of convergence reinforces the general finding they have in common, in this case, the undoing effect of positive experiences. Such convergence also increases confidence in the concept, which is important when applying this work to real life.

In other words, there are several reasons to believe that positive experiences make a difference for relational as well as individual well-being. First, in chapter 2, we saw that happiness and satisfaction involve having positive and meaningful experiences, respectively. Next, chapter 4 showed how it is possible to facilitate greater well-being by increasing the frequency of positive self-esteem moments. In this chapter, we encountered information suggesting that the same general rules concerning the dynamic nature of self-esteem apply to relational satisfaction. And now we know that all of these processes seem to be reciprocal in the way that self-fulfilling prophecies tend to be.

Therefore, it stands to good reason and some empirical support that we can use this information to construct thought activities that should have a positive impact on relational well-being. Further, it is likely that continuing them over time could undo relational damage and even trigger an upward relational cycle that parallels the one associated with positive emotions. Finally, due to the reciprocal nature of self-esteem in relationships, such healthy activity could positively affect the participants' self-esteem as well, especially because being valued as a person affects one's sense of worth.

The thought activity in Box 6.1a and Box 6.1b, called "Making the Positive Count in Relationships," is one possibility to consider. It is based on the blessings or good things exercise mentioned in chapter 5 and was first suggested to me in a class I teach on positive psychology. Some students, many of whom were raising families or approaching midlife, began trying the positive therapeutic activities developed in this field in their own work but with a creative twist. Instead of doing the activities as individuals, which was the case in the research on this type of activity, they included their families. Two ways of using this approach seem most common. One is to take the family through the activity at dinner time when its members often talk with each other about the events of the day. The other seems to be to use the method as a couple, usually later in the evening, perhaps before bed.

At one point in her relationship with her partner, M suffered a prolonged period of distress made worse by a chronic pain condition. Eventually, her negativity spilled over into the relationship. When the pain was medically relieved, she suddenly saw the toll the negativity generated by feeling less worthy and being less competent took on the relationship. She realized that she had been constantly taking the frustrations of the situation out on her partner through such hurtful behavior as blame and criticism, though never to the point of abuse. This realization occurred when he told M that he felt all of the criticism and blame meant that she no longer loved him and that the only solution he could think of to end their obvious mutual unhappiness was a divorce.

The latter part of his reaction, it turned out, was not at all true. M did indeed love her partner—very deeply, in fact. But the additional stress of prolonged pain she was feeling created a tipping point for her self-control that affected self-esteem in a negative way. Not only did it drop to lower levels, but the downward momentum generated by these negative ways of thinking, experiencing, and acting had affected the relationship as well. At some point the self-fulfilling nature of troubled self-esteem triggered off, or at least contributed to, a downward cycle in the relationship. The result of this development was, of course, that both people were suffering and so was the relationship, a situation that often occurs for couples when one partner suffers a chronic pain condition. Faced with this new challenge of living, M found herself dealing with a full-blown self-esteem crossroads of a relational type.

Fortunately, she remembered working on her personal self-esteem issues using the techniques concerning worthiness and competence in our work together as client and therapist. Having increased awareness from that process and realizing just how much of her life was at stake here, M became highly motivated to do whatever she could to make things good and right interpersonally. Consequently, M asked her partner to participate in the couple's version of the positive activity previously described. They agreed to try it at the rate of every evening for a month before making the decision of whether to separate.

Although there were rough times, the negative trajectory was corrected. In addition, since they were now focusing on positive experiences, both individuals came to see that the relationship was still important to each of them. As the number of positive experiences increased over time, the tone of the relationship took an upward turn, just as Fredrickson and the Gottmans might have predicted it would. In fact, the relationship became more enjoyable and meaningful than it had been in years. Things between M and her partner were still in need of attention, to be sure, but the relationship was good enough for both to be able to give it the time and nurturing it needed to recover. Not only did they stay together, but they began to grow (expand) again as a couple as well as individuals, which suggests a synergistic effect between healthy self-esteem and flourishing relationships, just as the research on happiness and relationships would suggest.

This anecdotal information does not substitute for actual published work supporting the practice, though it is consistently reported and should not be dismissed. However, the concept is based on the recognized therapeutic activities that have been shown to help both clinical and general populations in everyday life, and its practice is grounded in related work. Consequently, I present it for consideration. Again, a thought activity might be helpful as an exercise and can be included in a journal as well. It begins with an example using our client in Box 6.1a which is followed by a blank form in Box 6.1b.

Box 6.1a

THOUGHT ACTIVITY: MAKING THE POSITIVE COUNT IN RELATIONSHIPS

At dinner, the end of the day, or at least later into it, list several positive feelings, experiences, events, or interactions you had with your loved one(s) and describe what makes them good. Then, take turns sharing the three items with each other and why each one is positive. Remember, small positive events are especially valuable as they may help the brain to recognize and focus more on the good relational things that come our way in life. Similarly, recreating positive things and events in our minds through reflection, writing, and sharing may also rekindle and reinforce the positive affect associated with well-being and help facilitate change.

A. Positive feeling, experience, event, or interaction you had in relation to the other today.
   1. *My spouse/partner bought one of my favorite foods for me today.*
   2. *We made each other laugh a lot today.*
   3. *I made a comment today and realized that it hurt his feelings. We had a long talk about it. I came to understand and apologized. We hugged and felt closer to each other.*

B. Reflection on what makes each one of the previously listed events positive, valuable, important, or good.
   1. *The fact that my partner was thinking about me in a nice way without me even being around is good because it shows that he cares about me. That makes me feel special, valued, and worthy as a person.*
   2. *After all this time and even after some rough spots, we can still make each other laugh. Being free, spontaneous, and having fun together is good because it is relaxing (broadens attention), opens up new possibilities (the potential to build), and makes us want to spend more time together (action tendency).*
   3. *Although difficult, realizing my lack of thoughtfulness was causing problems in the relationship was a good thing because now I know how that happens. This awareness makes it possible to do something better, such as setting the positive goal of making sure that we have at least one positive relational experience together every day!*

Box 6.1b

Thought Activity: Making the Positive Count in Relationships

At dinner, the end of the day, or at least later into it, list several positive feelings, experiences, events, or interactions you had with your loved one(s) and describe what makes them good. Then, take turns sharing the three items with each other and why each one is positive. Remember, small positive events are especially valuable as they may help the brain to recognize and focus more on the good relational things that come our way in life. Similarly, recreating positive things and events in our minds through reflection, writing, and sharing may also rekindle and reinforce the positive affect associated with well-being and help facilitate change.

A. Positive feeling, experience, event, or interaction you had in relation to the other today.

1. _____

   _____

2. _____

   _____

3. _____

   _____

B. Reflection on what makes each one of the previously listed events positive, valuable, important, or good.

1. _____

   _____

2. _____

   _____

3. _____

   _____

SELF-ESTEEM AND SPIRITUALITY: A LARGER SENSE OF CONNECTION

Most of the work on self-esteem in an interpersonal context focuses on couples. However, some work involves connecting self-esteem to larger human communities, something Ryff and Singer (1998) described as social coherence in their model of mental health. For example, terror management theory placed self-esteem near the heart of what might be the largest form of community, namely, religion. Some people may find that there is a connection between self-esteem and religion to be surprising, but it should not be. Remember, John Milton used the term in one of the greatest religious epics of all time: *Paradise Lost* (Milton, 1667/1931). In fact, research showing a link between self-esteem and religion has been around for decades, though it does not seem to receive as much attention as it deserves in books on self-esteem or mental health in general.

Although it is more complex than meets the eye, it is possible to use this information to better understand this final connection between authentic self-esteem, being in touch with something larger than the self, and overall well-being. On one hand, a very substantial body of work indicates that there is a positive connection between self-esteem and religiosity. For example, some studies have found that those who believe in religion have higher self-esteem, better psychological adjustment, greater mental health, fewer physical health problems, a stronger sense of community, and longer lives than those who do not (Koenig, 1997). On the other, some very powerful cross-cultural work on religion and self-esteem indicates that the two are only connected in countries that are characterized by a high degree of religiosity in general, suggesting social support is the real factor giving rise to these positive outcomes (Gebauer, Sedikides, & Neberich, 2012). Therefore, our last question becomes, what are we to make of the connection between self-esteem, religiosity, and well-being?

Religiosity, of course, concerns the way one goes about expressing his or her spirituality, not just what religion one happens to observe. Masters and Bergin (1992) did some of the groundbreaking research in this area that is still highly relevant today. Perhaps their most important finding to always keep in mind when thinking about a connection between self-esteem and religion is that it is absolutely necessary to distinguish between two very different forms of religiosity before doing anything else in this area.

One is called *extrinsic religiosity* and is not a very attractive way of being religious because it only involves giving lip service to spiritual beliefs or, even worse, using them for self-serving ends. Extrinsic religiosity usually is seen in religious hypocrisy, for instance, which often takes the form of going to church, temple, mosque, or some other form of religious community on appropriate days but ignoring the customs, values, and morals of the religion the rest of the week. Unfortunately, extrinsic religiosity is also associated with a number of negative or unhealthy characteristics. They include such things as close-mindedness, rigidity, compulsiveness, and a tendency to be overly strict or judgmental toward others.

Indeed, extreme forms of extrinsic religiosity may even be associated with severe psychopathology. Some of the more notorious cult leaders, certain well-documented cases of sexual serial killers, and many terrorists or others who know no limits to imposing their vision of religion on other people exhibit this type of religiosity. Truly, it is destructive to authentic self-esteem, relationships, and well-being. Without question, this form of worship provides a false, self-serving sense of worthiness and is a thing to be avoided.

Intrinsic religiosity is just the opposite. Here people do their best to honor their beliefs in their daily lives without taking their views to extremes or inflicting them on others. This type of religiosity is usually associated with the more desirable phenomena previously mentioned concerning mental health and well-being. Intrinsic religiosity is also connected to authentic self-esteem in a way that we have already seen. For instance, although religions vary in many ways, they do hold some values in common, such as those that are found in the work on virtues (Peterson & Seligman, 2004) mentioned earlier. After all, what major religion does not admire or advocate such things as wisdom, a sense of humanity, moderation, social justice, or transcendence? Thus, in addition to the type of support a community of like-minded people offers during difficult times, those who are intrinsically religious can also be expected to have a higher degree of authentic self-esteem at least insofar as their competence and worthiness involve honoring these values.

Of course, it is also possible to hold these values and try one's best to live up to them without being religious in the formal sense. In fact, some of the most compassionate and virtuous people I know live this way. Moreover, the virtues and values listed in the VIA project also came from some secular sources, such as Aristotle's vision of the good life. Thus, I prefer the term *spirituality* to that of intrinsic religiosity, because spirituality is more inclusive: It allows the connection between the individual and humanity to be either religious or secular, as in the concept of a human spirit.

In either case, the connections between authentic self-esteem and spirituality (broadly defined) may be best seen in their similarities. For instance, believing in something larger than the self may buffer one's identity when it is threatened by negative personal and interpersonal events, and so does the protective function of self-esteem as it shields people from the full force of life's individual or relational setbacks and losses. Spirituality encourages us to strive to be better people, and so does the expansion function of self-esteem as it helps people move toward healthier levels of awareness and behavior. Spirituality provides one with a sense of direction when facing a challenge of living, and so does authentic self-esteem because it always involves making the worthier choice at these points in life. Finally, spirituality is associated with healthy relationships, such as ones characterized by mutual respect, care, and support, and, as we have just seen in this chapter, so is authentic self-esteem.

These connections do not mean, of course, that there are no differences between religious and secular approaches to self-esteem. Providing one lives his or her religion intrinsically rather than extrinsically, it is probably fair to say that a religious path toward authentic self-esteem is a smoother one, all things considered equal. After all, most religions have strong injunctions against many things that damage authentic self-esteem and simultaneously offer support for some things that enhance it. In the end, however, there appears to be only one path to authentic self-esteem, and it involves competently facing the challenges of living in ways that are worthy of a fully functioning human being and doing so over time. Consequently, the point is not whether a religious or secular road is the better one to take when it comes to self-esteem and well-being. Rather, it is important to ask what might be helpful to someone on either path, since both will face similar challenges to their competence and worthiness as a person.

Whether completely secular, intrinsically religious, or spiritual in the sense just mentioned, I can offer two final suggestions to help develop authentic self-esteem in ways that are likely to increase well-being. The first one involves building a self-esteem action plan around a theme or context that is clearly and meaningfully connected to the larger human community. For example, in chapter 5, M could have decided to do volunteer work to access the worthiness-based sources of self-esteem. Selecting a volunteer organization of intrinsic interest to her, in this case standing up for the rights of others, also involves the virtue of social justice, which connects her to the larger human community as well. As long as the choice is based on intrinsic values, this spiritual dimension of a self-esteem action plan could be executed in a religious or secular context, such as working through a church or with a lay organization concerned with human rights.

The second suggestion is actually a recommendation. It is aimed at helping people keep in mind the importance and value of authentic self-esteem by providing a set of guidelines. Such *condensed findings*, if I may call them that, offer food for thought, material for discussion, and suggestions for developing authentic self-esteem in everyday life. They are offered in Box 6.2, and it is hoped that they may even provide a meaningful degree of support when facing a challenge of living related to self-esteem.

A SENSE OF CLOSURE WITH PROMISE

It is only fitting to visit M one last time in closing this look at authentic self-esteem and its connection to well-being. By now, it should be apparent that there were several good reasons to present her particular self-esteem story. For one thing, M was selected because her experience showed how self-esteem, or rather a lack of it, is involved in various personal and interpersonal problems that often affect well-being for people in general. For another, her capacity to remember early childhood experiences connected to the development of self-esteem helped reveal important aspects of both factors that define and create it. In addition to demonstrating common problems with both competence and worthiness to which most people may relate, M's story also helped us better understand how subtly the development of problematic self-esteem may begin even when facing relatively minor challenges of living.

Box 6.2

Ten Guidelines to Authentic Self-Esteem

1. Remember that authentic self-esteem is based on both competence and worthiness.
2. Realize that authentic self-esteem is earned, not given, as we feel good by doing good.
3. Understand that life's challenges can sometimes be valuable self-esteem opportunities.
4. Appreciate how authentic self-esteem is tied to worthwhile values and basic virtues.
5. Know that in the long run, doing the right thing is best for self-esteem and well-being.
6. Reframe thoughts that diminish a sense of worth to break free of self-esteem traps.
7. Use problem-solving abilities to create positive competence-based self-esteem moments.
8. Try to always have a self-esteem action plan in process.
9. Learn to pay more attention to the importance of self-esteem in relationships: It matters.
10. Understand that authentic self-esteem helps one connect to something larger than the self.

Another valuable dimension of M's experience was her ability to increase her self-awareness, which is usually necessary for growth. Not only did she learn much about how the self-protective function of self-esteem helped shaped her life, but she also showed an increasing interest in the willingness to embrace possibilities associated with its second function, namely, self-expansion. Approaching such a tipping point often signals that a person is ready for change, and some people interested in a book on self-esteem may be in a similar situation. Perhaps learning about how another person went through the process of change may be helpful to them or to those who work with them.

In short, M's story helps reveal important dimensions about how self-esteem traps develop, why it is difficult to break free of them later in life, and how to do so personally as well as relationally. Of course, I could have selected someone with more serious self-esteem problems to illustrate its nature. For instance, it is possible to describe the self-esteem dynamics of a narcissist or an antisocial personality, both of whom often have massive problems finding authentic self-esteem because of the defensiveness and instability associated with these conditions. Although such examples might have made for fascinating reading, they would also have taken the book in a far more clinical direction than was intended here, though I have done that elsewhere (Mruk, 2013a). Since the goal of this book is to reach more people, using an example of more typical self-esteem problems provides a better opportunity to show how it is possible for almost anyone to increase authentic self-esteem and interpersonal, as well as individual, well-being.

In the end, of course, M did not go on to live happily ever after. Hardly anyone does. But during therapy, it became clear to both of us that she was very much engaged in making her life better. For example, when M faced a crisis of competence, she often remembered the work she did with the problem-solving method to increase her competence. Similarly, as she continued to deal with her worthiness-based self-esteem traps though cognitive restructuring, M began to have a more realistic sense of her worth as a person. By the end of treatment, she showed signs of shifting from low to medium self-esteem. Providing M continues to develop and use a self-esteem action plan, there is no reason she cannot continue to reach higher levels of self-esteem and well-being.

If she does, it is reasonable to expect that the duration of her flow states will increase over time. Positive emotions should become more frequent in her personal and interpersonal life. She may even focus more of her time and energy on activities that reflect her own intrinsic values. Making them more central in this way is likely to increase her sense of purpose and satisfaction. Although such positive upward cycles are never permanent, they do make life better. Perhaps even more, M should be able to look forward to increasing her sense of connection to others, including her child, partner, and community. How could anyone realistically ask for more when it comes to the link between self-esteem and well-being?

Aron, A., Ketay, S., Riela, S., & Aron, E. (2008). How close others construct and reconstruct who we are and how we feel about ourselves. In J. Wood, A. Tesser, & J. Holmes, (Eds.), *The self and social relationships* (pp. 209–229). New York: Psychology Press.

Aune, K. S., & Wong, N. C. (2002). Antecedents and consequences of adult play in romantic relationships. *Personal Relationships, 9,* 279–286.

Baldwin, M. (2006). Self-esteem and close relationship dynamics. In M. Kernis (Ed.), *Self-esteem issues and answers: A sourcebook of current perspectives* (pp. 359–366). New York: Psychology Press.

Bartoletti, M. (2008). Effectiveness of Mruk's self-esteem change program on psychological and physiological measures of well-being. *Dissertation Abstracts International: Section B. Sciences and Engineering, 68*(8-B), 5557.

Baumeister, R. F., Campbell, J. D., Krueger, J. I., & Vohs, K. D. (2003). Does high self-esteem cause better performance, interpersonal success, happiness, or healthier lifestyles? *Psychological Science in the Public Interest, 4,* 1–44.

Baumeister, R., Smart, L., & Boden, J. (1996). Relation of threatened egotism to violence and aggression: The dark side of self-esteem. *Psychological Review, 103,* 5–33.

Bednar, R., Wells, G., & Peterson, S. (1989). *Self-esteem: Paradoxes and innovations in clinical theory and practice.* Washington, DC: American Psychological Association.

Bekoff, M., & Pierce, J. (2009). *Wild justice: The moral lives of animals.* Chicago: University of Chicago Press.

Berenson, K., & Downey, G. (2006). Self-esteem and rejection sensitivity in close relationships. In M. Kernis (Ed.), *Self-esteem issues and answers: A sourcebook of current perspectives* (pp. 367–373). New York: Psychology Press.

Berger, P. L. (1967). *The sacred canopy.* New York: Doubleday.

Branden, N. (1969). *The psychology of self-esteem.* New York: Bantam.

Buhrmester, D., Furman, W., Wittenberg, M. T., & Reis, H. T. (1988). Five domains of interpersonal competence in peer relationships. *Journal of Personality and Social Psychology, 55,* 991–1008.

Burns, D. (1980). *Feeling good: The new mood therapy.* New York: Signet.

Casey, B. J., Somerville, L. H., Gotlib, I. H., Ayduk, O., Franklin, N. T., Askren, M. K., . . . Shoda, Y. (2011). Behavioral and neural correlates of delay of gratification 40 years later. *Proceedings of the National Academy of Sciences, 108,* 14998–15003.

Churchill, S. D., & Mruk, C. J. (2014). At the crossroads of humanistic psychology and positive psychology: Practicing what we preach. *American Psychologist, 69,* 90–92.

Coopersmith, S. (1967). *The antecedents of self-esteem.* San Francisco, CA: Freeman.

Crocker, J., & Park, L. E. (2004). The costly pursuit of self-esteem. *Psychological Bulletin*, *130*, 392–414.

Csikszentmihályi, M. (1990). *Flow: The psychology of optimal experience*. New York: Harper & Row.

DeHart, T., Tennen, H., Armeli, S., Todd, M., & Afflect, G. (2008). Drinking to regulate negative romantic relationship interactions: the moderating role of self-esteem. *Journal of Experimental Social Psychology*, *44*, 527–538.

Diener, E., & Diener, M. (1995). Cross-cultural correlates of life satisfaction and self-esteem. *Journal of Personality and Social Psychology*, *68*, 653–663.

Donnay, D. A. C., Morris, M. L., Schaubhut, N. A., & Thompson, R. C. (2004). *Strong Interest Inventory* (Rev. ed.). Palo Alto, CA: Consulting Psychologists Press.

Duckworth, A. L., Steen, T. A., & Seligman, M. E. P. (2005). Positive psychology in clinical practice. *Annual Review of Clinical Psychology*, *1*, 629–651.

Durand, V. M., & Barlow, D. H. (2015). Abnormal psychology: An integrative approach (7th ed.). Pacific Grove, CA: Thompson-Wadsworth.

D'Zurilla, T. J., & Goldfried, M. R. (1971). Problem-solving and behavior modification. *Journal of Abnormal Psychology*, *78*, 107–126.

Ellis, A., & Harper, R. (1977). *A new guide to rational living*. North Hollywood, CA: Wilshire.

Epstein, S. (1979). The ecological study of emotions in humans. In P. Pliner, K. R. Blankstein, & I. M. Spigel (Eds.), *Advances in the study of communication and affect: Vol. 5. Perception of emotions in self and others* (pp. 47–83). New York: Plenum.

Erikson, E. (1983). *The life cycle completed*. New York: Norton.

Fischer, C. (1986). *Individualizing psychological assessment*. Belmont, CA: Wadsworth.

Fredrickson, B. L. (2002). Positive emotions. In C. R. Snyder & S. J. Lopez (Eds.), *Handbook of Positive Psychology* (pp. 120–134). New York: Oxford.

Fredrickson, B. L. (2013). Positive emotions broaden and build. *Advances in Experimental Psychology*, *47*, 1–53.

Fredrickson, B. L., Mancuso, R. A., Branigan, C., & Tugade, M. M. (2000). The undoing effect of positive emotions. *Motivation and Emotion*, *24*, 237–258.

Gagne, F., Khan, A., Lydon, J., & To, M. (2008). When flattery gets you nowhere: Discounting positive feedback as a relationship maintenance strategy. *Canadian Journal of Behavioral Science*, *40*(2), 59–68.

Gebauer, J. E., Sedikides, C., & Neberich, W. (2012). Religiosity, social self-esteem, and psychological adjustment: On the cross-cultural specificity of the psychological benefits of religiosity. *Psychological Science*, *23*, 158–160.

Gottman, J. (1995). *Why marriages succeed or fail*. New York: Fireside.

Hakim-Larson, J., & Mruk, C. (1997). Enhancing self-esteem in a community mental health setting. *American journal of Orthopsychiatry*, *67*, 655–659.

Harkin, B., Webb, T. L., Chang, B. P. I., Prestwich, A., Conner, M. T., Kellar, I., . . . Sheeran, P. (2016). Does monitoring goal progress promote goal attainment? A meta-analysis of the experimental evidence. *Psychological Bulletin*, *142*, 198–229.

Harter, S. (1999). *The construction of the self: A developmental perspective*. New York: Guilford.

Helliwell, J., Layard, R., & Sachs, J. (2016). *World happiness report 2016, update* (Vol. 1). New York: Sustainable Development Solutions Network.

Hepper, E. G., Sedikides, C., & Cai, H., (2013). Self-enhancement and self-protection strategies in China: Cultural expressions of a fundamental human motive. *Journal of Cross-Cultural Psychology, 44*, 5–23.

Hobbes, T. (1994). Of the natural condition of mankind, as concerning their felicity, and misery. In Curley, E. (Ed.), *Leviathan: With selected variants from the Latin edition of 1668* (pp. 99–104). Indianapolis: Hackett Publishing. (Original work published 1651)

Hunt, B. (2010). Women and self-esteem. In M. Guindon (Ed.), *Self-esteem across the lifespan* (pp. 191–204). New York: Routledge.

Jackson, M. (1984). *Self-esteem and meaning: A life historical investigation.* Albany: State University of New York.

James, W. (1983). *The principles of psychology.* Cambridge, MA: Harvard University Press. (Original work published 1890)

Kernis, M. H. (2003). Optimal self-esteem and authenticity: Separating fantasy from reality. *Psychological Inquiry, 14*, 83–89.

Keyes, C. L. (2002). The mental health continuum: From languishing to flourishing in life. *Journal of Health and Social Behavior, 43*, 207–222.

Kiecolt-Glaser, J. K., Glaser, R., Cacioppo, J. T., MacCallum, R. C., Snydersmith, M., Kim, C., & Malarkey, W. B. (1997). Marital conflict in older adults: Endocrinological and immunological correlates. *Psychosomatic Medicine, 59*, 339–349.

Koenig, H. G. (1997). *Is religion good for your health? The effects of religion on physical and mental health.* Binghamton, NY: Haworth Pastoral.

Krauthammer, C. (1990, February 5). Education: Doing bad and feeling good. *Time Magazine*, p. 78.

Kristjansson, K. (2013). *Virtues and vices in positive psychology: A philosophical critique.* New York: Cambridge University Press.

Leary, M. R. (2004). The sociometer, self-esteem, and the regulation of interpersonal behavior. In R. F. Baumeister & K. D. Vohs (Eds.), *The handbook of self-regulation: Research, theory, and application* (pp. 373–391). New York: Guilford.

Leary, M. R. (2008). Functions of the self in interpersonal relationships: What does the self actually do? In J. Wood, A. Tesser, & J. Holmes (Eds.), *The self and social relationships* (pp. 95–115). New York: Psychology Press.

Leary, M. R., & MacDonald, G. (2003). Individual differences in self-esteem: A review and theoretical integration. In M. R. Leary & J. P. Tangney (Eds.), *Handbook of self and identity* (pp. 401–418). New York: Guilford.

Lyubomirsky, S. (2001). Why are some people happier than others? The role of cognitive and motivational processes in well-being. *American Psychologist, 56*, 239–249.

Maslow, A. H. (1970). *Motivation and personality.* New York: Harper & Row. (Original work published 1954)

Masters, K., & Bergin, A. (1992). Religious orientation and mental health. In J. Schumaker (Ed.), *Religion and mental health* (pp. 221–232). New York: Oxford.

McKeon, R. (Ed.). (1941). *The basic works of Aristotle.* New York: Random House.

Mead, G. H. (1934). *Mind, self, and society.* Chicago: University of Chicago Press.

Menard, A., & Offman, A. (2009). The interrelationships between sexual self-esteem, sexual assertiveness and sexual satisfaction. *Canadian Journal of Human Sexuality, 18*, 35–45.

Milton, J. (1931). Paradise lost. In F. A. Patterson (Ed.), *The works of John Milton.* New York: Columbia Press. (Original work published 1667)

Milton, J. (1950). Apology against a pamphlet. In C. Brooks (Ed.), *Complete poetry and selected prose of John Milton*. New York: Modern Library. (Original work published 1642)

Mischel, W., Ebbesen, E., & Zeiss, A. (1972). Cognitive and attentional mechanisms in delay of gratification. *Journal of Personality and Social Psychology, 21,* 204–218.

Mruk, C. (1995). *Self-esteem: Research, theory, and practice.* New York: Springer Publishing Company.

Mruk, C. (2008). Positive psychology and positive therapy: Implications for practitioners. *Ohio Psychologist, 55,* 16–17.

Mruk, C. (2013a). Self-esteem and positive psychology: Research, theory, and practice (4th ed.). New York: Springer Publishing Company.

Mruk, C. (2013b). Self-esteem, relationships, and positive psychology: Concepts, research, and connections. In M. Hojjat & D. Cramer (Eds.), *Positive psychology of love* (pp. 149–161). New York: Oxford University Press.

Mruk, C., & Skelly, T. (2017). Is self-esteem absolute, relative, or functional? Implications for cross-cultural psychology. *The Humanistic Psychologist, 45,* 313–322.

Murphy, B., & Dillon, C. (2011). *Interviewing in a multicultural world* (4th ed.). Pacific Grove, CA: Brooks/Cole.

Murray, S. (2008). Risk regulation in relationships: Self-esteem and the if-then contingencies of interdependent life. In J. Wood, A. Tesser, & J. Holmes (Eds.), *The self and social relationships* (pp. 3–25). New York: Psychology Press.

Myers, D. (2000). *The American paradox: Spiritual hunger in an age of plenty.* New Haven, CT: Yale University Press.

O'Brien, E. J., Bartoletti, M., & Leitzel, J. D. (2006). Self-esteem, psychopathology and psychotherapy. In M. H. Kernis (Ed.), *Self-esteem: Issues and answers: A sourcebook of current perspectives* (pp. 306–315). New York: Psychology Press.

O'Brien, E. J., & Epstein, S. (1983, 1988). MSEI: The multidimensional self-esteem inventory. Odessa, FL: Psychological Assessment Resources.

Park, L., Crocker, J., & Vohs, K. (2006). Contingencies of self-worth and self-validation goals: Implications for close relationships. In K. Vohs & E. Finkel (Eds.), *Self and relationships: Connecting intrapersonal and interpersonal processes* (pp. 84–103). New York: Guilford.

Peterson, C., & Seligman, M. (2004). *Character strengths and virtues: A handbook and classification.* Oxford: Oxford University Press.

Pope, A., McHale, S., & Craighead, E. (1988). Self-esteem enhancement with children and adolescents. New York: Pergamon.

Prochaska, J. O., & Norcross, J. C. (1994). Systems of psychotherapy: A transtheoretical analysis (3rd ed.). Pacific Grove, CA: Brooks/Cole.

Pyszczynski, T., Greenberg, T., & Goldberg, J. L. (2003). Freedom versus fear: On the defense, growth, and expansion of self. In M. R. Leary & J. P. Tangney (Eds.), *Handbook of self and identity* (pp. 315–343). New York: Guilford.

Random acts of kindness day. Retrieved January 10, 2017 from DaysoftheYear. com: https://www.daysoftheyear.com/days/random-acts-of-kindness-day/.

Raskin, J. D. (2002). Constructivism in psychology: Personal construct psychology, radical constructivism, and social constructionism. In J. D. Raskin & S. K. Bridges (Eds.), *Studies in meaning: Exploring constructivist psychology* (pp. 1–25). New York: Pace University Press.

Robbennolt, J. K. (2008). Apologies and medical error. *Clinical Orthopedics and Related Research, 467,* 376–382.

Rodewalt, F., & Tragakis, M. W. (2003). Self-esteem and self-regulation: Toward optimal studies of self-esteem. *Psychological Inquiry, 14,* 66–70.

Rogers, C. (1961). *On becoming a person.* Boston, MA: Houghton Mifflin.

Rosenberg, M. (1965). *Society and the adolescent self-image.* Princeton, NJ: Princeton University Press.

Rosenberg, M., & Simmons, R. G. (1971). Black and white self-esteem: The urban school child. *Social Psychological Implications IX, Rose Monograph Series.*

Ryff, C. D., & Singer, B. (1998). The contours of positive human health. *Psychological Inquiry, 9,* 1–28.

Schmitt, D. P., & Allik, J. (2005). Simultaneous administration of the Rosenberg Self-Esteem Scale in 53 nations: Exploring the universal and culture-specific features of global self-esteem. *Journal of Personality and Social Psychology, 89,* 623–642.

Sciangula, A., & Morry, M. M. (2009). Self-esteem and perceived regard: How I see myself affects my relationship satisfaction. *Journal of Social Psychology, 149,* 143–158.

Sedikides, C., Gaertner, L., & Cai, H. (2015). On the panculturality of self-enhancement and self-protection motivation: The case for the universality of self-esteem. In A. J. Elliott (Ed.), *Advances in motivation science* (Vol. 2, pp. 185–241). New York: Academic Press.

Seligman, M. E. P., Steen, T. A., Park, N., & Peterson, C. (2005). Positive psychology progress: Empirical validation of interventions. *American Psychologist, 5,* 410–421.

Seligman, M. E. P. (1990). *Learned optimism: How to change your mind and your life.* New York: Simon & Schuster.

Sheldon, K. M., Elliot, A. J., Kim, Y., & Kasser, T. (2001). What is satisfying about satisfying events? Testing 10 candidate psychological needs. *Journal of Personality and Social Psychology, 80,* 325–339.

Smelser, N. J. (1989). Self-esteem and social problems: An introduction. In A. M. Mecca, N. J. Smelser, & J. Vasconcellos (Eds.), *The social importance of self-esteem* (pp. 1–23). Berkeley: University of California Press.

Stinson, D. A., Logel, C., Zanna, M. P., Holmes, J. G., & Cameron, J. J. (2008). The cost of lower self-esteem: Testing a self-and-social-bonds model of health. *Journal of Personality and Social Psychology, 94,* 412–428.

Tafarodi, R. W., & Swann, W. B., Jr. (1995). Self-liking and self-competence as dimensions of global self-esteem: Initial validation of a measure. *Journal of Personality Assessment, 65,* 322–342.

Tafarodi, R. W., & Vu, C. (1997). Two-dimensional self-esteem and reactions to success and failure. *Personality and Social Psychology Bulletin, 23,* 626–635.

Tice, D. (1993). The social motivations of people with low self-esteem. In R. Baumeister (Ed.), *Self-esteem: The puzzle of low self-regard* (pp. 37–54). New York: Plenum.

Trzesniewski, K. H., Robins, R. W., Roberts, B. W., & Caspi, A. (2004). Personality and self-esteem development across the life span. In P. T. Costa & I. C. Siegler (Eds.), *Psychology of aging* (pp. 163–185). Amsterdam, The Netherlands: Elsevier Science.

Vaillant, G. E. (1998). *Wisdom of the ego.* Cambridge, UK: Harvard University Press.

White, R. (1959). Motivation reconsidered: The concept of competence. *Psychological Review, 66,* 297–333.

Winnicott, D. (1953). Transitional objects and transitional phenomena. *International Journal of Psychoanalysis, 34*, 89–97.

Zeigler-Hill, V., Campe, J., & Myers, E. (2009). How low will men with high self-esteem go? Self-esteem as a moderator of gender differences in minimum relationship standards. *Sex Roles, 61*, 491–500.

Zilcha-Mano, S. (2017). Is the alliance really therapeutic? Revisiting this question in light of recent methodological advances. *American Psychologist, 72*, 311–325.

Box 1.1b

THOUGHT ACTIVITY: APPRECIATING THE TWO COMPONENTS OF AUTHENTIC SELF-ESTEEM

1. Describe an experience or situation that involved feeling worthwhile as a person.

   _____

   _____

   _____

   _____

2. Describe an experience or situation in which you were competent at something.

   _____

   _____

   _____

   _____

3. Describe an experience or situation in which you were competent at doing something worthy.

   _____

   _____

   _____

   _____

4. Summarize what these experiences show you about authentic self-esteem.

_____

_____

_____

_____

(Modified from: Mruk, C. (2013a). Self-Esteem and positive psychology: Research, theory, and practice (4th ed.). New York, Springer Publishing Company.)

Box 2.1b

THOUGHT ACTIVITY: APPRECIATING THE VALUE OF POSITIVE EMOTIONS

1. Describe the situation in which the positive emotion emerged.

_____

_____

_____

_____

2. Describe the types of things you experienced, including thoughts as well as feelings during the time the positive emotion occurred.

_____

_____

_____

_____

3. Describe the value of seeing, feeling, and acting in the ways that occurred while or after feeling the positive emotion and how they could help increase well-being in the future.

_____

_____

_____

_____

4. Repeat as desired until the ability to identify and appreciate ordinary positive things in life increases enough to affect one's sense of well-being or to at least offset some negative emotions.

_____

_____

_____

Box 3.1b

THOUGHT ACTIVITY: IDENTIFYING POTENTIAL SOURCES OF SELF-ESTEEM

1. First, describe an experience, interaction, or situation that involves competence, worthiness, or both. Then reflect on it as a potential source of self-esteem in your life.

a. Being Valued (Worthiness)

_____

_____

_____

_____

b. Being Virtuous (Worthiness)

_____

_____

_____

_____

c. Having a Positive Influence on Something (Competence)

_____

_____

_____

_____

d. Personal Achievements (Competence)

_____

_____

_____

_____

(Modified from: Mruk, C. (2013a). Self-Esteem and positive psychology: Research, theory, and practice (4th ed.). New York, Springer Publishing Company.)

Box 3.2b

THOUGHT ACTIVITY: DOMAINS OF SELF-ESTEEM

A. Worthiness-Based Domains

1. Being Connected: Relationships in your life that seem to bring a sense of acceptance/worth.

_____

_____

2. Physical Attractiveness: Things about your appearance or presence that receive compliments.

_____

_____

3. Morality and Virtue: Times in life or areas in which you maintain a high degree of integrity.

_____

_____

B. Competence-Based Domains

1. Problem-Solving Abilities: Your particular skills and abilities.

_____

_____

2. Autonomy and Control: Areas in life where you have a voice, influence, or make decisions.

_____

_____

3. Physical Integrity: Positive abilities based on your age, gender, and abilities.

_____

_____

Box 4.1b

THOUGHT ACTIVITY: BREAKING FREE OF SELF-ESTEEM WORTHINESS TRAPS
WITH NICC

A. Begin by identifying a situation, event, or interaction that lessened your
   sense of worthiness as a person. Briefly describe it here:

   _____

   _____

B. Then use the following steps to break out of any self-esteem traps created
   by faulty patterns.

Step 1: Notice	**Step 2: Identify**	**Step 3: Correct to Counteract**
negative thoughts you have about what happened.	the traps unrealistic thoughts created by using the list.	the problematic thoughts to make them more accurate by writing out realistic alternatives.
a.	a.	a.
b.	b.	b.
c.	c.	c.
d.	d.	d.

C. Finally, focus on the change that occurs at the end of the process. People
   who do so usually find that things are not as bad as they thought and that a
   more realistic view reduces an unnecessary loss of worthiness or suffering.
   Remember, the key to this "worthiness tool" is practice.

(Modified from: Mruk, C. (2013a). Self-Esteem and positive psychology: Research, theory, and
practice (4th ed.). New York, Springer Publishing Company.)

Box 4.2b

THOUGHT ACTIVITY: INCREASING COMPETENCE WITH PROBLEM-SOLVING SKILLS

Basic 4-step problem-solving method: Move through the steps and be sure to detail the plan.

Step 1: Problem	Step 2: Solutions	Step 3: Consequences
a.	a.	a.
	b.	b.
	c.	c.
	d.	d.

Step 4: (Best) Plan

a. _____

b. _____

c. _____

d. (etc.) _____

(Modified from: Mruk, C. (2013a). Self-Esteem and positive psychology: Research, theory, and practice (4th ed.). New York, Springer Publishing Company.)

Box 4.3b

THOUGHT ACTIVITY: SELF-DIRECTED SELF-ESTEEM ASSESSMENT FORMAT

A. Worthiness Domains

   1. **Being Connected:** This domain involves the quality of relationships in your life as that has been shown to be connected to both self-esteem and happiness in general.

     A. Greatest Strength: _____

     B. Area to Work On: _____

     C. Importance: _____

   2. **Physical Attractiveness:** This item concerns how important you think physical attractiveness is for you in general.

     A. Greatest Strength: _____

     B. Area to Work On: _____

     C. Importance: _____

   3. **Morality and Virtue:** This dimension focuses on a very important aspect of positive self-regulation: the ability to comport yourself in a way that is virtuous or worthy of a fully functioning person.

     A. Greatest Strength: _____

     B. Area to Work On: _____

     C. Importance: _____

B. Competence Domains

   1. **Problem-Solving Abilities:** This item deals with your ability to function well at work, manage finances, run a home, and deal with the tasks of living.

     A. Greatest Strength: _____

     B. Area to Work on: _____

     C. Importance: _____

2. **Autonomy and Control**: This domain concerns the degree to which you have the ability to have a voice in regard to situations or environments, including social ones, in your life.

   A. Greatest Strength: _____

   B. Area to Work on: _____

   C. Importance: _____

3. **Physical Integrity:** This dimension involves the extent to which your physical potentials and limitations affect your ability to do the things you want or need to do.

   A. Greatest Strength: _____

   B. Area to Work on: _____

   C. Importance: _____

Box 5.1b

Thought Activity: Making Positive Self-Esteem Moments Count

1a. Note a self-esteem moment you experienced and identify which
    components were present.

_____

_____

_____

1b. Describe which source(s) of self-esteem the experience reflects and why it
    is good.

_____

_____

_____

2a. Note a self-esteem moment you experienced and identify which
    components were present.

_____

_____

_____

2b. Describe which source(s) of self-esteem the experience reflects and why it
    is good.

_____

_____

_____

3a. Note a self-esteem moment you experienced and identify which
    components were present.

_____

_____

_____

3b. Describe which source(s) of self-esteem the experience reflects and why it
    is good.

_____

_____

_____

_____

Box 5.2b

THOUGHT ACTIVITY: IDENTIFYING INTRINSIC VALUES AS WELL-BEING
STRENGTHS

1a. I feel that I am most meaningfully engaged or satisfied with life when I?
(*Describe* activity.)

_____

1b. This activity reflects the value of _____? (*Identify* a positive value related to
well-being.)

_____

1c. This value is one of my strengths because _____. (*Write* a reason
supporting this observation, such as why the quality is valuable.)

_____

2a. I feel that I am most meaningfully engaged or satisfied with life when I?
(*Describe* activity.)

_____

2b. This activity reflects the value of _____? (*Identify* a positive value related to
well-being.)

_____

2c. This value is one of my strengths because _____. (*Write* a reason
supporting this observation, such as why the quality is valuable.)

_____

3a. I feel that I am most meaningfully engaged or satisfied with life when I?
(*Describe* activity.)

_____

3b. This activity reflects the value of _____? (*Identify* a positive value related to
well-being.)

_____

3c. This value is one of my strengths because _____. (*Write* a reason
supporting this observation, such as why the quality is valuable.)

_____

Box 6.1b

THOUGHT ACTIVITY: MAKING THE POSITIVE COUNT IN RELATIONSHIPS

At dinner, the end of the day, or at least later into it, list several positive feelings, experiences, events, or interactions you had with your loved one(s) and describe what makes them *good*. Then, take turns sharing the three items with each other and why each one is positive. Remember, small positive events are especially valuable as they may help the brain to recognize and focus more on the good relational things that come our way in life. Similarly, re-creating positive things and events in our minds through reflection, writing, and sharing may also rekindle and reinforce the positive affect associated with well-being and help facilitate change.

A. Positive feeling, experience, event, or interaction you had in relation to the other today.

    1. _____

    _____

    2. _____

    _____

    3. _____

    _____

B. Reflection on what makes each one of the above events positive, valuable, important, or *good*.

    1. _____

    _____

    2. _____

    _____

    3. _____

    _____

Page references for figures are indicated by *f*, for tables by *t*, and for boxes by *b*.